ORTHO'S All Abou

Attracting Birds

Written by Michael McKinley

Meredith® Books
Des Moines, Iowa

Ortho® Books
An imprint of Meredith® Books

All About Attracting Birds
Contributing Editor: Sally Roth
Contributing Technical Editors:
   Craig Tufts, National Wildlife Federation
   Stephen R. Kress, Ph.D., Cornell University and
      the National Audubon Society
Contributing Writer: John V. Dennis
Art Director: Tom Wegner
Assistant Art Director: Harijs Priekulis
Copy Chief: Catherine Hamrick
Copy and Production Editor: Terri Fredrickson
Book Production Managers: Pam Kvitne,
   Marjorie J. Schenkelberg
Contributing Copy Editor: Barbara Feller-Roth
Contributing Proofreaders: Mary Duerson, Elizabeth Neils,
   Fran Gardner, Barbara J. Stokes, JoEllyn Witke
Contributing Illustrator: Mike Eagleton
Contributing Photo Stylist: Peggy Johnston
Indexer: Donald Glassman
Electronic Production Coordinator: Paula Forest
Editorial and Design Assistants: Kathleen Stevens,
   Karen Schirm

Meredith® Books
Editor in Chief: James D. Blume
Design Director: Matt Strelecki
Managing Editor: Gregory H. Kayko
Executive Ortho Editor: Larry Erickson

Director, Retail Sales and Marketing: Terry Unsworth
Director, Sales, Special Markets: Rita McMullen
Director, Sales, Premiums: Michael A. Peterson
Director, Sales, Retail: Tom Wierzbicki
Director, Sales, Home & Garden Centers: Ray Wolf
Director, Book Marketing: Brad Elmitt
Director, Operations: George A. Susral
Director, Production: Douglas M. Johnston

Vice President, General Manager: Jamie L. Martin

Meredith Publishing Group
President, Publishing Group: Christopher M. Little
Vice President, Finance & Administration: Max Runciman

Meredith Corporation
Chairman and Chief Executive Officer: William T. Kerr
Chairman of the Executive Committee: E.T. Meredith III

Thanks to
   Duncraft, Becky Jerdee, Colleen Johnson, and Spectrum
   Communication Services, Inc.

Photographers
   (Photographers credited may retain copyright ©
   to the listed photographs.)
L = Left, R = Right, C = Center, B = Bottom, T = Top
Cliff Beittel: 66, 86C
Ernest Braun: 56
Les Campbell/Positive Images: 29T
Carolyn Chatterton: 20, 32, 70C, 79B, 89B
Richard Day/Daybreak Imagery: 10T, 10B, 15BC, 19T, 25T,
   26, 30, 33T, 33B, 36T, 58, 59B, 60-1, 60-5, 63, 65, 70T,
   71T, 78C, 78B, 81B, 82T, 91C
Jerry Howard/Positive Images: 47C, 57
Adam Jones: 31, 88T
Steven W. Kress: 46C
Scott Leonhart/Positive Images: 60-3
Bill Marchel: 35T, 47T, 74B, 75T, 90B
Steve & Dave Maslowski: 6, 7, 11T, 11B, 13, 15BL, 18,
   22T, 34, 35B, 36B, 37T, 37B, 46B, 48, 49T, 49B, 53T,
   59T, 60-4, 62B, 64T, 64B, 67C, 68T, 70B, 71C, 73T,
   73B, 75B, 76C, 77B, 79T, 79C, 80T, 80C, 80B, 82B,
   83T, 84T, 85B, 86T, 86B, 87T, 87C, 89T, 89C, 90T, 91B
Joe McDonald: 5TL, 5TR, 14, 19B, 72C, 88C
Michael McKinley: 22B
Charles W. Melton: 5B, 28, 54B, 55, 60-2, 68B, 69T, 69B,
   75C, 81C, 83C, 84C, 87B, 88B, 90C, 91T
Anthony Mercieca: 29B, 41BRC, 71B, 74T, 74C, 77C, 78T,
   81T, 83B, 85C
James H. Robinson: 84B
Rob & Ann Simpson: 12, 60BR, 68C
Ty Smedes: 60-6, 72B
Hugh P. Smith, Jr.: 25B, 38, 41BL, 41BLC, 41BR, 47B, 50,
   51, 53B, 54T, 62T, 67T, 67B, 69C, 72T, 73C, 76T, 76B,
   77T, 82C, 85T
Pam Spaulding/Positive Images: 46T
Steve Struse: 42, 44, 45, 52
Connie Toops: 4, 15BR, 40
Tom Vezo: 8T, 8B, 9T, 9B, 92

On the cover: Male Northern Cardinal in a crabapple tree.
   Photograph by Adam Jones.

All of us at Ortho® Books are dedicated to providing you
with the information and ideas you need to enhance your
home and garden. We welcome your comments and
suggestions about this book. Write to us at:
   Meredith Corporation
   Ortho Books
   1716 Locust St.
   Des Moines, IA 50309–3023

If you would like more information on other Ortho
products, call 800-225-2883 or visit us at www.ortho.com

BIRDS IN THE WILD 4

BIRDS IN THE GARDEN 18

PROVIDING FOOD 34

PROVIDING WATER 48

PROVIDING HOUSING 58

GALLERY OF BIRDS 66

4

BIRDS IN THE WILD

Provide nesting places, food, water, and shelter similar to the resources birds seek in the wild to make your yard more inviting to birds. This Eastern Bluebird, a cavity-nesting species, has a family safely tucked inside the hole in an old apple tree. The bluebird box shown on page 5 is an artificial version of the natural cavities that bluebirds seek for nesting.

Birds add life to all our landscapes, from our backyards to our favorite wild places. Whether it's warblers filling a spring morning with birdsong, goldfinches flashing their colors in the late summer garden, or a flock of busy chickadees enlivening a dull winter's day—birds bring music, color, and motion every day. No matter what the season, birds make it a pleasure to be in the garden or gaze out a window. Birds are also a vital part of nature's balance. By devouring millions of insects, they help plants stay healthy; by eating seeds, they help keep weeds under control; by swallowing berries and storing acorns, they ensure that new dogwoods, oaks, and other plants will emerge from the seeds they spread.

When you want to learn how to attract birds to your garden, birds in the wild are your best teachers. Observing them as they forage for food or find water, collect nesting materials, and seek shelter allows you to create similar surroundings in your garden so that birds feel at home. A garden with a reliable and abundant supply of food, water, and shelter quickly attracts birds that otherwise would need to range far afield to manage the necessities of everyday life.

Pay attention to wild birds and you'll quickly discover clues to what they find appealing. Watch a woodpecker at work, and you'll see that these birds seek trees to glean for hidden insects and larvae; observe a Song Sparrow and you'll notice that brushy cover is paramount to attracting these engaging birds, which spend much of their time on the ground. The first chapter of this book, "Birds in the Wild" (pages 4–17), will help you become familiar with the differing needs of birds, from the essentials of food and water to the vital need for protective cover. You'll also learn about the habitats of birds, so you can create similar conditions in your garden.

In the wild, plants fulfill nearly all birds' needs. "Birds in the Garden" (pages 18–33) will help you choose the right plants and arrange them in your yard to create the most attractive bird habitat. You will also find tips for attracting hummingbirds. The all-you-can-eat buffet of a feeding station, detailed in the third chapter, "Providing Food" (pages 34–47), is guaranteed to attract delightful customers, from quiet juncos to flashy jays, which you will enjoy watching up close. In "Providing Water" (pages 48–57), you'll learn how to supply birds with water for sipping and splashing. In "Providing Housing" (pages 58–65), you'll find instructions for encouraging birds to nest in your yard. And the "Gallery of Birds" (pages 66–91) introduces you to 75 favorite backyard birds with specific information on attraction techniques for each.

HELPING BIRDS MEET NEEDS

Like all creatures, birds require four basic things to survive: food, water, protection from the elements and danger, and a place to raise their young safely. You can match those needs for many birds in your home landscape, but some birds are so specialized that you may never see them in your garden. Unless you have a large pond, for instance, don't count on attracting ducks!

The birds of our gardens have adapted to life near humans because they are comfortable in that habitat and can fill some or all of their basic needs there. We can offer niger seed to goldfinches, which seek out similar small, oil-rich seeds in the wild, or offer birdhouses to bluebirds, chickadees, and other cavity nesters to imitate a natural hole in a tree. These birds are quick to take advantage of the benefits humans offer.

This book will help you understand the natural lives of birds and discover resources that encourage them to live in or regularly visit your landscape.

Bluebirds, wrens, chickadees, and other cavity nesters are quick to investigate any inviting entrance to a potential homesite. Nest boxes that mimic the size and safety of natural cavities are eagerly accepted.

FOOD

Birds choose their menu from a variety of natural resources. Foods they eat include insects, spiders, and worms; nuts and seeds; berries and other fruits; flower nectar; tree sap; the tender buds of shrubs and trees; eggs and nestlings taken from other birds' nests; other birds; fish and small animals; and carrion they scavenge.

The bill of a bird is a clue to its food preference. Seedeaters, such as the Northern Cardinal, finches, grosbeaks, towhees, sparrows, juncos, the Indigo Bunting, and the Pine Siskin, have strong, cone-shaped bills with an angled cutting edge at the base, well adapted to cracking hard, dry seeds. These birds depend on seeds year-round, although they also eat insects. Their diet contains a greater proportion of insects in spring and early summer, when seeds are relatively scarce and the birds' developing young need the concentrated protein that insects provide. Other birds' bills are also adapted to their major food preferences. Some birds, such as crows and ravens, have bills that can tackle practically any kind of food.

Sight, hearing, and even flight habits also play a part in food-finding. The Purple Martin and other swallows, which feed on the wing, eat almost nothing but flying insects. The hearing of the Eastern Screech-Owl is so acute that it can detect the location of a mouse in total darkness. The American Robin can actually see the subtle movements of earthworms when it peers at the surface of the soil. Much is still to be discovered about the sensory perception of birds and how it affects food preferences.

SEASONAL CHANGES IN DIET

Although some birds have narrowly specialized food preferences, most of the birds attracted to our gardens eat a wide variety of foods throughout the year. Diet is determined by the availability of food and the energy requirements of the season. When insects are plentiful, birds feast on the protein-rich morsels. When wild fruits or garden fruits ripen, birds are quick to move in for a share. The Yellow-rumped Warbler and Tree Swallow, two birds that appear to be exclusive insect eaters because of their bill and family grouping, actually switch to bayberry, poison ivy berries, and other fruits in fall. Even the woodpeckers with their strong, chisel-shaped bills eat wild grapes and Virginia creeper berries in fall and readily eat sumac in winter. Nearly all birds require plant food at some time of the year, as it helps them build fat for migration.

BILLS, BEAKS, AND DIET

The shape of a bird's bill (called a beak in the case of birds of prey) helps to determine the type of food it eats. Seedeaters, such as this Northern Cardinal, have strong, conical bills with sharp edges for cracking open hard seed coats. The slender, down-curved bill of the Brown Creeper reaches into crevices of tree bark for insects and their larvae. Woodpeckers have strong, chisel-shaped bills for probing and chipping into wood for insects. The slender bills of American Robins and other thrushes are suited for eating mostly insects and soft fruits and berries. Purple Martins, swallows, and phoebes scoop insects out of the air with wide-gaping bills surrounded by bristles. American Kestrels and other birds of prey have sharp, curved beaks to tear flesh.

WATER

All birds need to consume water to survive. A few desert birds not ordinarily found in gardens can extract all the water they need from hard, dry seeds, but most birds must make frequent trips to a source of open water to drink.

In nature, birds find their water in rivers, ponds, lakes, and streams, as well as less obvious sources: raindrops, puddles, dewdrops, snow, and, in some cases, sap, nectar, and moist fruits. In the garden a birdbath or pool may attract a greater variety of birds than any food we provide.

Birds vary in the way they approach water. Some strong fliers, such as swallows, dip into water while on the wing. Open expanses that allow unrestricted flight are most attractive to them. Species that dwell in mature forests or thickets, such as the Varied Thrush and Eastern Towhee, approach water slowly, in a long, cautious process. They prefer water right next to the protective cover of shrubs and trees. Most garden birds like a water source somewhere between the two extremes, far enough from surrounding vegetation to offer surveillance against a surprise attack yet close enough for refuge. These birds often approach water by perching in a nearby tree. Then they drop down for a quick drink and a splash, followed by preening on a tree branch. It is not unusual for birds to return for one or two more baths before settling down to dry and preen themselves.

Most songbirds can't swim, so they seek shallow water with secure footing. Watch birds in the wild and you'll see that the edges of streams where shallow water pools around rocks or over gravel are the favored spots for drinking and bathing—not the deep, fast-running parts of the stream. Look around your neighborhood after a rain, and you'll notice birds gathering at puddles on lawns, patios, or streets. In these impromptu natural birdbaths, they can safely quench their thirst or clean their feathers.

VITAL REFRESHMENT

Once birds find a reliable source of water, whether in the wild or in your backyard, they will return day after day. Birds seek water in all seasons. If you live in a cold-winter area, notice how rapidly birds flock to the melting edge of a puddle or pond. Summer droughts are a critical time for birds, and during spring and fall migration, birds are also quick to zero in on a source of water.

The sound of moving water is irresistible to birds, whether the water music is made by

The sound of running water quickly attracts birds to bathe and drink. Songbirds such as this Northern Cardinal seek out shallow pools with sure footing and nearby cover for perching, preening, or escape. Even when bathing, birds remain alert to possible danger.

raindrops or a waterfall. Sit quietly near a brook, and you may spot tanagers, the Rose-breasted Grosbeak, and other beautiful songbirds arriving for their daily bath. A light rain also brings out many birds to enjoy the bounty of falling water. Tiny hummingbirds fly back and forth through misty rain to cleanse their feathers; American Robins and other thrushes often hop about during a gentle shower instead of retreating to shelter.

Any bird, from the ordinary American Robin to the seldom-seen Orange-crowned Warbler, is great fun to observe at its bath. As you watch wild birds at water, try to identify what most attracts them to a bathing or drinking spot so that you can create a similar situation in your garden. "Providing Water" (pages 48–57) is filled with ideas for ways to offer water that will delight you and birds.

PROTECTIVE COVER

The bright-colored male Scarlet Tanager flaunts his plumage from the treetops where he dwells, but his mate—who incubates the eggs without her gaudy partner's assistance—wears yellow-green feathers, which blend perfectly with the foliage around the nest.

Because birds depend on flight for safety, they are most vulnerable when they are "grounded" to rest, feed, or nest. A bird's protection is intimately connected with the kind of plants that it seeks for cover. Scarlet Tanagers find protection high in a tree from the hot sun, the cold wind and rain, or the prying eyes of predators. California Quail take cover on the ground under a clump of grass or in the low branches of a shrub. The color of a bird's plumage, its defense posture, and its way of getting from one place to another also protect it from enemies.

CAMOUFLAGE ARTISTS

Feathers insulate birds from the damp and cold, retain vital body heat, and make efficient flight possible. Although some birds, such as the male Northern Cardinal and the male Baltimore Oriole, sport colorful plumage year-round, the color of a bird's feathers most often reflects the kind of plant cover it seeks for protection. The streaky golden feathers of a Yellow Warbler are difficult to distinguish from the sun-dappled foliage of willows, a preferred habitat. The dusky browns of thrushes blend well with the leaves and grasses they frequent under shrubs close to the ground. The plumage of females of nearly all bird species blends with their environment so they are camouflaged at the nest.

The postures that birds adopt when danger threatens also help protect them. Many birds freeze in place when they spot a predator. Nuthatches remain stock-still on tree

trunks and branches so that they look like a part of the tree. Sapsuckers, woodpeckers, and the Brown Creeper hitch around to the far side of a sheltering tree trunk. Sparrows, doves, and quail hunch down among grasses to escape notice.

HIDING PLACES

Foot structure is an example of a physical attribute that helps determine where a bird seeks cover. Songbirds, which include many of the birds we see in our gardens, are referred to by scientists as perching birds. They have a specialized foot structure in which three toes point forward and one points backward to oppose them. This makes them adept at clinging to cylindrical objects such as twigs, branches, or grass stems.

Birds with more specialized adaptations are more limited in their habitat. Quail and other ground birds also have three toes pointed forward and one backward, but their feet and legs are strong, with long, clawed toes. Although fast fliers for short distances, quail are such good runners and walkers that they take to the air only when necessary. Their preferred cover is close to the ground in grasses and shrubs. Woodpeckers, nuthatches, and creepers, which cling to and climb on trees, have long toes and sharp claws that help them grip rough vertical surfaces, and stiff tails for bracing. Most woodpeckers have four long toes—two pointing forward, two backward—ideal for navigating tree trunks.

Only the most determined predator would dare risk the dastardly spines that surround the homesite of this Cactus Wren. Birds often seek rosebushes, hawthorns, pyracantha, and other prickly plants for nesting or for resting out of harm's way.

When a hawk or other predator approaches, birds seek safety according to their particular strengths. A Red-breasted Nuthatch may halt motionless, for example, whereas a woodpecker may circle behind a tree trunk and a Dark-eyed Junco may dart to the nearest dense vegetation. Except for birds of open country, most rarely stray far from dense cover, because their lives depend upon quick evasion. Areas dense with weeds or brush are frequently occupied by birds, although you may not notice them at first because birds become silent and still as you approach. Deadfalls—brush piles formed by fallen branches and trees—are also favored, because the tangle of branches prevents hawks or cats from gaining access.

Protective cover is also vital when birds are sleeping or waiting out bad weather. Conifers and other evergreens, as well as dense deciduous plants, shelter roosting birds from predators and wind, rain, and snow. Titmice, chickadees, woodpeckers, bluebirds, and other cavity nesters often seek nighttime roosts in birdhouses and cavities in trees or utility poles.

Screech-owls seek a daytime roost safe from harassment by jays. At night, when owls are on the wing, conifers often shelter sleeping songbirds.

MOVING ABOUT SAFELY

For most birds, protective cover plays a large role in the way they move about.

The California Quail, a bird of open spaces, travels rapidly on foot, spending a lot of time in narrow corridors through grass and shrubs where it can easily duck to one side for cover. The Mourning Dove prefers an unobstructed path for its swift flight back and forth between foraging on open ground and perching on higher lookouts. Most birds, however, spend almost all their time hidden inside the cover of dense vegetation. Instead of flying or walking across wide-open spaces, they travel short distances from one stand of plants to another. Watch birds as they cross open areas and you will notice that most are highly wary. The American Tree Sparrow, for instance, twists and turns erratically as it dashes across an open space.

Inside protective vegetation, birds tend to occupy preferred vertical layers. Natural habitat provides a multilayered approach to bird protection, especially in wooded areas where mature trees rise above mid-layers of younger trees and shrubs, a lower layer of herbaceous plants, and a bottom layer of fallen leaves and ground-hugging plants. Birds that spend most of their time on or near the ground—sparrows,

juncos, towhees—move safely through the bottom layer of leaf litter or grass, brush piles, and low-growing plants. Thrushes, the Bushtit, buntings, thrashers, the Gray Catbird, and other mid-level birds find cover in brush, shrubs, and young trees. High in the treetops are orioles, tanagers, kinglets, and warblers.

Birds may occasionally move vertically from one level to another, as when a Baltimore Oriole pursues a flying insect to the ground or searches for nesting materials. A few species, including chickadees and titmice, range freely from the heights to ground level and back again in the eternal search for food. In general, birds spend most of their time moving about more or less horizontally through their preferred layer.

Brown birds such as this Hermit Thrush often nest near the ground, where their plumage makes them hard to see among leaves.

A PLACE TO RAISE YOUNG

The female Ruby-throated Hummingbird builds one of the smallest nests of all birds. Only two nestlings, hatched from eggs the size of small beans, occupy the dainty 1¼-inch lichen-studded cup.

Few other bird activities captivate bird lovers as much as courtship, nest-building, and the raising of young. Birds are highly active during the entire process, and their behavior is fascinating to observe as they compete for mates, engage in courtship, and care for their families. The artistry and resourcefulness that many birds display in nest-building are among their most interesting habits. Watching birds during this time gives us a new appreciation for their busy lives and offers more clues for tempting them to our garden with food, cover, and nesting materials.

COURTSHIP

For most birds, courtship season gets under way in spring. Owls, the Mourning Dove, and bluebirds are the early birds, setting up housekeeping in the waning days of winter, which can be disastrous should a late storm or severe cold snap arrive. In spring, after migrants return, nesting hits a peak that continues through early summer. Goldfinches and waxwings are the late bloomers: They begin nesting in summer, after most other birds have already fledged their new families.

Male birds select a nesting territory and claim their property rights by singing loudly from various trees, shrubs, or utility pole perches along the boundaries. The same perches around the perimeter of the nesting territory are often used day after day as the bird makes its rounds. The song functions as an advertisement for a female mate at first, and also as a warning against trespassing rivals of the same species. Males continue singing after they find a mate, so pay attention to the birds you hear: They announce who is nesting in the area.

In spring, male goldfinches, tanagers, and other birds that wear duller plumage in winter now don the vivid colors of their breeding, or nuptial, plumage. The flashy colors are used in courtship displays in which the male bird contorts himself to show off his prettiest parts. The male Scarlet Tanager, for example, lets his wings droop to show his brilliant red back to impress a potential mate. Hummingbirds engage in amazing aerial courtship displays in which they swing like a pendulum or perform loops before an admiring mate, their iridescent feathers flashing in the sun.

Birds of many species form a pair-bond that lasts for life, but not all are monogamous. Hummingbirds are notoriously fickle, with the male and female joining just long enough for mating to take place; after that it's on to the next for the male, while the female goes off to rear the young alone. But for most birds, courtship and mating are the prelude to several weeks of dedicated family life.

If you see an American Robin collecting a bill full of mud in your garden, watch where the bird goes next: She's likely building a nest on a branch or in a crotch of a nearby tree. Two or three broods each year, with three to six nestlings in each batch, help make the American Robin one of the most successful songbirds.

NEST-BUILDING

Nests generally are built in the same kind of cover that adults use the rest of the year for protection: dense branches or undergrowth, thorns, prickly foliage, leafy treetops, and tangled vines. The Song Sparrow and other ground-nesting birds seek undisturbed areas where they can build a well-camouflaged nest among leaves, grasses, or other low plants. Woodpeckers chisel out nesting holes in tree trunks, and many other birds use abandoned woodpecker holes as well as other natural cavities for nesting.

Bird nests are marvels of construction yet surprisingly inconspicuous. The most familiar kind is the cup nest. Attached to a limb or nestled in the crotch of branches, the nest may contain hundreds of pieces of material skillfully woven together. The nest of the American Goldfinch is so tightly woven that it will hold water. If the parents are unable to return to the nest in time to protect the nestlings from rain, the young may drown.

Twigs, plant stems and fibers, and grass are basic building materials. An astonishing array of other items may be added: leaves, plant down, bark, silk from spiderwebs and cocoons of caterpillars, pine needles, moss, feathers, and animal hair. Pets as well as wild and domestic animals are common subjects of hair raids, and titmice are even reported to pull hair from human heads! Birds also prize human-made materials, such as string, yarn, tissue, and strips of plastic.

Mud puddles are popular places during nesting season for several species that use mud to build nests, such as the American Robin and the Barn Swallow.

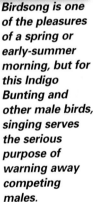

Birdsong is one of the pleasures of a spring or early-summer morning, but for this Indigo Bunting and other male birds, singing serves the serious purpose of warning away competing males.

REARING YOUNG

Convenient sources of food and water are vital in choosing where to raise a brood. Nestlings can eat up to one and one-half times their weight each day. Feeding them requires many energy-draining trips for parents, so the parents' food demands are higher than usual. Protein-rich insects are the prime food for both nestlings and parents during this time. Parent birds glean insects for their young from the same places they find their own food: trees, shrubs, and other plants; in leaf litter and grass; in crevices in bark or in wood; or in the air.

The most dangerous period in a bird's life is from the time it is an egg to when it is a young bird that can fend for itself. Cold wind and rain are especially hazardous. Depredation of eggs and young by other birds and animals takes a heavy toll too. Songbirds often leave the nest before they are able to fly, which means they are vulnerable to predators during the two or three days they perfect their new skills near ground level. Their parents settle the youngster in nearby protective cover, which is imperative at this stage of a bird's life. Young birds must be able to take shelter quickly and move about without exposing themselves to predators.

Nesting generally ends by midsummer. Young birds soon experience their first change of season—and the shift in food that comes with it, especially in cold-winter areas, where seeds and berries replace the insects of warmer months. Some join in small groups to forage in a winter feeding territory; others band together for migration.

Nest materials reflect the habitat of the parent birds, which helps to disguise the nest among its similar surroundings. Like the males of many species, this Eastern Towhee, a dweller of woods' edge and brushy thickets, leaves nest-building and incubation to the female but assists in feeding the young.

RANGE

The broad geographical area within which all the individuals of a bird species are found is called the range of that species. Scientists have compiled years of observation by thousands of people across the continent (many of them interested amateurs) to form range maps for each bird species found in North America. In the "Gallery of Birds" beginning on page 66, you will find a range map for each bird described. The boundaries of a range are the result of many factors. Birds' movements are limited by physical obstacles, such as mountain ranges or large bodies of water over which they cannot or will not fly. Climate, too, plays an important role in determining range. For example, the aridity of a desert might prove inhospitable to one species; another may not be able to withstand cold conditions.

SEASONAL RANGES

A bird's environment is seldom static. Ranges can shift, dwindle, or grow because of broad environmental changes, such as long-term climatic shifts or human alteration of the landscape. Ranges can also change seasonally. The needs of a bird frequently change with the season; the specialized needs of nesting and breeding are often quite different from the generalized needs of simply surviving. The habitat itself may undergo dramatic changes as the seasons progress, and these changes affect available food, water, and plant cover.

Therefore, a species of bird can have more than one range, depending on the season. These ranges are usually called the breeding range and the winter range, although these terms are a bit misleading. Some birds move into their winter range soon after breeding is over, in late summer. Most birds stay around their breeding range for some time after the young have left the nest. In an area where the breeding and winter ranges coincide and a species of bird may be seen year-round, the bird is known as a permanent resident.

Some birds, such as the Northern Cardinal, are permanent residents in a fairly restricted area where individuals spend their entire lives, both summer and winter. Birds of other species roam from one place to another as conditions and competition change locally. Only when the movement of a bird is regular and seasonal, however, is it called migration. The distance of migration may be short and local, as is the twice-annual hike of some quail up and down a mountainside. Or it may be dramatically long, such as the Purple Martin's yearly flight to South America. Migration is an interesting specialization developed over eons.

When migratory birds are in their summer, or breeding, range, they are called summer residents; when in their winter range, they are called winter residents. When traveling in between, in an area not their summer or winter range, they are called transients.

Some birds, such as these Tree Swallows, gather together in enormous numbers during migration. When they reach a good feeding and resting area, ducks, geese, Purple Martins, robins, and other tired and hungry travelers pour in to spend hours, days, or weeks refueling for the next leg of the journey.

On the map above, the migratory pattern of the American Robin illustrates the move south from its summer breeding range (gold) to the winter range (purple). Robins are seen in their permanent range (green) year-round, although individual birds are different—in fall, summer residents move south, and birds of more northern climes migrate south to replace them.

HABITAT

The broad area on a map showing the range of a species is only a generality, with some areas in which populations are large and other areas in which that species may not be found at all. *Habitat* is a more specific description of where a bird lives.

As we have seen, birds use many resources to survive. Their choice of habitat depends on the ways they are adapted to find and use the resources they need.

Plants are a most important habitat resource for birds. Plants are a source of food, yielding fruits, berries, nuts, seeds, greens, sap, and nectar. Living plants and their decomposing remains are the main food of most insects, which in turn compose a large part of the diet of most birds. Plants provide nesting sites and comfortable resting spots, protecting birds from unfavorable climatic conditions. They also provide a refuge from predators so that birds may venture forth to eat and drink.

Plants are so important in the life of birds that the plant communities a bird prefers are often the basis for how we define its habitat.

THE RICHEST HABITATS: EDGES, LAYERS, STAGES

Ecologists classify habitats in many different ways, from broad categories, such as forest or open country, to specific subdivisions of enormous variety, such as the edge of a forest pool or a desert oasis. The widest variety of bird species, as well as the greatest number of individual birds, live in transitional places where one type of habitat changes to another.

EDGES: One category of such transitional places—where one habitat changes horizontally across space into another kind of habitat— is called an *edge*. The brushy edge of a woods, for example, hosts more birds than the forest itself or the field that the edge gives way to. Where edges occur, some birds from the habitats on both sides move freely into the edge to feed or seek shelter; others spend most of their time in the edge habitat itself.

In the edges between habitats, plant life is often more diverse and complex than in the habitats on either side. For example, besides the grasses and flowers of an open field, its edge may also include shrubs, young trees, and other plants typical of the woodland it borders. This plant diversity both expands and concentrates resources for birds.

LAYERS: A second category of transitional space—where habitat changes vertically through space—is the *layer*. Birds tend to favor certain strata, or heights, in which they spend most of their time. These layers divide resources and expand the number of species an area can support. In a forest, for example,

birds that prefer life on the ground can share the same space with birds of shrubs and low understory trees and birds of the treetops, while all use different resources. A forest is one example of layering, but birds divide into similar layers in open-country habitats too.

STAGES: Besides edges and layers, a third type of transitional place with a rich, diverse bird population—a *mid-successional stage*— occurs as a place changes over time. In nature, disturbed land (such as burned or cleared forest) grows and evolves through predictable stages, beginning with a pioneer invasion of annual plants to eventually reach a stable community called a *climax*. Climax communities generally support fewer, more specialized species, whereas earlier stages often resemble edge habitats with a greater variety. For example, in the East, an *old field* in a mid-successional stage on its way to climax forest is one of the richest of all bird habitats, full of the seed-producing wildflowers and the berry-producing shrubs beloved by many birds.

Hedgerows—linear strips of shrubs, trees, and herbaceous plants along fence lines at the margins of agricultural fields and roads—are well-known as productive bird habitats, and with good reason. Think of hedgerows as old fields that birds planted themselves with their favorite food plants, in a concentrated area.

Often found in the edge habitats that mark the transitions between forest, field, and backyard, the Downy Woodpecker moves freely between woods and gardens. Diversity is high in edge habitats, which attract birds with tempting plants such as this mullein, with its bounty of seeds and insects.

BIRDS OF THE FOREST

The dark blue Steller's Jay of the West is secretive and shy in the forests in which it dwells, but it is a raucous presence at the bird feeder and in backyards, especially in winter.

Birds that dwell in forests have evolved to take advantage of the natural food, shelter, and nesting sites offered there. Pinecones, acorns, maple seeds, and other nuts and seeds feed many birds; insects in bark and on foliage nourish others. Living trees provide indispensable cover for resting and nesting. Dead trees and snags are vital nest sites and feeding places for woodpeckers and many other birds.

Some birds, such as the Pine Siskin, Purple Finch, and Varied Thrush, live in predominantly *coniferous forests* (conifers, such as pine or spruce, are mostly evergreen trees with needle-shaped leaves). Other birds are found mostly in *deciduous forests*—the Blue Jay, for example, inhabits the beech-maple forests of the Northeast or the drier oak-hickory forests of the Midwest. But many forest birds that are common in gardens reside in *mixed forests* that contain both evergreen coniferous and deciduous broad-leaved trees.

Many of the forest birds that frequent our gardens readily cross the spaces between broken forest and scattered trees to inhabit smaller woodlands or relatively open areas in winter. Other shy forest dwellers (many rarely seen around the home landscape) require many acres of uninterrupted forest. In the chart on pages 16 and 17, the birds listed as deep-forest dwellers are most likely to be found only in gardens that include trees and are close to a woodland.

VERTICAL LAYERS

A forest habitat is much more than trees. Under the tall forest canopy, the understory layers of small trees, shrubs, herbaceous plants, and leaf litter supply a series of vertical zones vital for supporting many different birds. Some birds are most often found high in treetops and on trunks. Small trees and shrubs provide critical nesting spots and food sources for others. Still other birds forage and nest in low shrubs and groundcovers, wildflowers, and leaf litter on the forest floor. If deer browse away most of the understory plants, or if overly neat humans clear them out, remove critical dead trees and brush piles, and rake leaves from the forest floor, birds disappear.

Birds may spend most of their time in one layer, such as the Scarlet Tanager of the treetops, or they may move among layers for the different resources each zone offers. For example, many birds use nesting material from all levels, such as moss, rootlets, grapevine bark, and dead leaves.

FOREST EDGES

Forest openings and margins—such as a space where trees have been logged, or a grassy meadow, or an expanse of bedrock or poor soil that doesn't support the demands of trees— are important edge formations.

At forest edges, where the shade-tolerant plants of the deep forest merge with the sun-loving plants of the opening, the vegetation is dense and varied. Some areas offer a greater variety of fruits and seeds, more insects that feed on the plants, and a wider choice of nesting sites and cover. Where dense forests border open country, you can usually find populations of birds from both habitats.

For forest-dwelling birds, an opening can mean increased danger as well as increased safety. Birds can be easily spotted by an airborne predator such as the Sharp-shinned Hawk, but they can spot ground-moving predators more easily than in dense forest. To minimize the risk, most birds spend their time at the margins of forest openings, making only quick forays into the treeless space.

Openings lend themselves well to this dash-and-hide movement. Whether openings are long and linear, such as a roadway or utility right-of-way, or closed and circular, such as a meadow or a forest pond, birds often use them as flight pathways to make their way through a broken forest, racing through the exposed spaces to the protection of woodland on the other side. Similarly, in a garden, open corridors of lawn, driveway, and paths allow birds to move quickly from place to place.

Bodies of water—lakes, ponds, or rivers— also create openings and attract birds to the water and food they provide. In the East, bottomland woods bordering a river or wide stream, with their dense thickets at the water's edge overhung with tall sycamores, elms, maples, and sweet gums, are attractive to birds such as the Baltimore Oriole, Red-headed Woodpecker, and Tufted Titmouse.

BIRDS OF OPEN COUNTRY

Birds that hunt on the wing, such as Purple Martins and other swallows, prefer open grasslands without obstructions to their flight. A few birds of open country, such as the Wrentit of the Pacific coast chaparral, almost never leave the cover of shrubs and prefer uninterrupted brushland. Most birds of open country that are common in gardens live in mixed brushland and grassland, in which patches of shrubs and small trees are interrupted by patches of wildflowers and grass. This complex mix of cover, feeding places, and nesting places has great appeal for many birds.

DIVERSITY IN OPEN COUNTRY

Abandoned agricultural fields in the East—in mid-successional stages with complex mixes of grasses, wildflowers, shrubs, and small trees—provide a variety of heights at which birds can forage, hide, and nest, as well as a profusion of rich food-bearing plants. Some birds found in old fields nest on the ground among grasses; others seek shrubs or tangled vines to hide their homes. Grasses and flowering plants such as sunflower, aster, and coneflower provide abundant seeds in fall and winter for sparrows, goldfinches, and other finches. Juniper, wild rose, blackberry, and hawthorn provide fruits and dense cover for other birds such as the Northern Cardinal, Northern Mockingbird, and Cedar Waxwing.

The dense evergreen shrubs of Pacific coast chaparral, the sagebrush of the western plains, and the mesquite and cactus scrub of the desert Southwest are dominated by shrubs and grasses; these areas lack the water necessary to support trees. Many birds make their homes in these areas. Some, such as the California Quail and Cactus Wren, are found only in these habitats. Other birds, such as the White-crowned Sparrow, House Finch, and Northern Mockingbird, are also found in moist brushlands as well as gardens.

THE EDGE IN OPEN COUNTRY: PROMINENCE, ISLAND, GROVE

In open country a prominence—a single tall tree, a utility pole, or even a fence post, for example—is a magnet for many kinds of birds, which use it for a singing perch, a lookout from which to watch for danger or scout for prey, and a nesting site. The Red-headed Woodpecker and bluebirds, which seek an unobstructed vantage point for vocalizing and feeding forays, quickly adopt an isolated perch in open spaces. The American Kestrel uses such a prominence for hunting observations.

The vegetation encouraged by the year-round water of rivers and streams and the springs and pools of desert oases creates dense islands and corridors of resources for many birds. Many of the birds that frequent forest openings are also found in the islands of refuge provided by groves of trees in open country. Birds that roam use groves as stopping-off places. Other birds use islands for the additional food and cover they provide.

Especially if you live in open country, bringing its mosaic of grassy stretches and clusters of shrubs, trees, or other vegetation into the garden makes your landscape inviting to birds of open spaces as well as birds of forest edges. A large property can include grassy meadows with rocky outcrops and islands of shrubs and trees. Even a smaller garden has room for an oasis. You'll find practical ideas for incorporating natural habitats into your garden in the next chapter.

In open country, high perches for singing, hunting, and scouting are often rare; even fence posts are valuable to many birds. This California Quail (far left) is on guard near a nest; the American Kestrel (center) waits for grasshoppers or other prey; the male Eastern Bluebird (right) keeps watch for passing insects and proclaims its territory with a song.

PREFERRED NATURAL HABITATS OF BIRDS

Here you will find the birds that are described in the "Gallery of Birds" (starting on page 66) categorized by the nine bird habitats described in this chapter—three kinds of habitat in open country and six kinds in forested country. In the next chapter, "Birds in the Garden," you will learn how to develop these habitats in the landscape around your home. Use this chart to help you analyze your property and its regional context, to help you

Bird	Open Country			Forest					
	Waterside Vegetation	Grove, Prominence	Mixed Brush, Grass	Margin on Open Country	Waterside Vegetation	Broken Forest, Openings	Deep Deciduous	Deep Coniferous	Deep Mixed
Bluebird, Eastern			■		■				
Bluebird, Western			■		■				
Bunting, Indigo	■				■		■		
Bunting, Lazuli	■			■	■		■		
Bushtit	■			■					
Cardinal, Northern	■	■		■	■				
Catbird, Gray	■	■			■	■			
Chickadee, Black-capped			■			■			
Chickadee, Chestnut-backed						■		■	■
Chickadee, Mountain			■					■	
Creeper, Brown			■		■		■	■	
Dove, Mourning		■	■		■		■	■	■
Finch, House			■	■					
Finch, Purple	■		■						
Flicker, Northern	■		■				■		■
Goldfinch, American			■	■	■		■		
Grosbeak, Evening		■					■		
Grosbeak, Rose-breasted			■		■			■	■
Hummingbird, Anna's	■					■	■		
Hummingbird, Costa's	■			■		■			
Hummingbird, Ruby-throated						■			
Hummingbird, Rufous					■		■		
Jay, Blue						■			
Jay, Steller's						■		■	■
Junco, Dark-eyed						■	■	■	■
Kestrel, American			■	■	■	■	■	■	■
Kinglet, Ruby-crowned			■		■				
Martin, Purple					■		■		■
Mockingbird, Northern	■								
Nuthatch, Red-breasted			■		■				
Nuthatch, White-breasted								■	■
Oriole, Baltimore							■	■	■
Oriole, Orchard	■		■			■	■		
Phoebe, Black	■		■			■			
Phoebe, Eastern	■					■			
Pigeon, Band-tailed	■					■			
Quail, California			■		■		■		
Redpoll, Common	■		■	■			■	■	■

predict which birds are most likely to appear there, and to begin deciding which kinds of habitat would be most appropriate for you to create or enrich.

Remember that, in general, garden birds are opportunistic. Many are specific about habitat during breeding but are willing to explore a surprisingly wide variety of habitats the rest of the year. Because a bird is listed as preferring a habitat on this chart does not mean it is exclusive to that habitat and won't be found elsewhere.

For easy reference the birds in this chart are presented alphabetically rather than in evolutionary order as in the "Gallery of Birds."

Bird	Open Country — Waterside Vegetation	Open Country — Grove, Prominence	Forest — Mixed Brush, Grass	Forest — Margin on Open Country	Forest — Waterside Vegetation	Forest — Broken Forest, Openings	Forest — Deep Deciduous	Forest — Deep Coniferous	Forest — Deep Mixed
Robin, American			■		■		■		
Sapsucker, Yellow-bellied						■	■		
Screech-Owls			■		■	■	■		
Scrub-Jay, Western			■	■			■	■	
Siskin, Pine			■		■				
Sparrow, American Tree	■			■					
Sparrow, Chipping	■			■					
Sparrow, Fox						■	■	■	■
Sparrow, Song	■		■	■					
Sparrow, White-crowned	■			■					
Sparrow, White-throated	■			■			■		
Swallow, Barn	■								
Swallow, Tree	■					■			
Swallow, Violet-green	■								■
Tanager, Scarlet							■		
Thrasher, Brown				■	■				
Thrasher, California	■			■					
Thrush, Hermit							■	■	■
Thrush, Varied						■		■	
Titmouse, Oak	■		■		■				■
Titmouse, Tufted			■				■	■	
Towhee, California				■					
Towhee, Canyon	■			■					
Towhee, Eastern	■			■	■		■		
Warbler, Orange-crowned						■	■	■	
Warbler, Yellow	■		■		■	■	■	■	
Warbler, Yellow-rumped			■	■	■		■		
Waxwing, Cedar	■		■	■	■		■		■
Woodpecker, Downy			■				■	■	
Woodpecker, Hairy						■	■	■	■
Woodpecker, Red-bellied					■		■		
Woodpecker, Red-headed	■		■				■		
Wren, Cactus	■			■					
Wren, Carolina			■		■	■	■		
Wren, House					■	■		■	■
Wren, Winter								■	■
Wrentit	■			■					
Yellowthroat, Common	■								

BIRDS IN THE GARDEN

Shrubs with tasty berries are guaranteed to bring birds to your garden. Berries that linger on the branches into fall and winter, such as those of the deciduous holly (Ilex) shown here, attract such birds as the Evening Grosbeak, a welcome surprise when it shows up on its irregular wanderings from the far north.

With their irrigated lushness, numerous flowering and fruiting plants of different heights, and mosaic of open spaces bounded by dense flower borders and shrubby hedges, our gardens often approach the complex diversity of habitats favored by many birds—without our even thinking about it. So imagine the success you will enjoy if you consciously offer the most diverse and abundant bird resources possible, arranged in a habitat or combination of habitats that appeals to the birds in your area that you most want to attract—and in a way that visually appeals to you too. Adopt the threefold strategy of diversity, abundance, and good fit, and you will enjoy the highest numbers and widest variety of preferred bird species around your home year-round.

THE GARDEN AS HABITAT

Rather than a mere collection of individual resources attractive to birds such as plants, feeders, birdbaths, and nest boxes, the most successful bird-attracting gardens are *habitats* in which the mix, configuration, placement, and timing of resources, their relationship to one another, and their relationship to the world "over the garden wall" are all as important as which resources are offered.

Look closely at birds in nature, and you can draw parallels between natural bird habitats and the resources you should offer around your home. For instance, they may appear different to human eyes, but nest boxes and tree cavities function in many of the same ways for certain birds. When you understand this relationship, the advantage of mounting nest boxes on posts and poles is obvious. And when you look closer at the habits of individual bird species, you learn a host of other details, such as where to place the box and how high it should be.

Drawing such parallels is a good technique for developing larger landscapes too. In the previous chapter, we showed how edges, multiple vertical layers, and mid-successional stages in the development of plant communities (such as old fields and hedgerows) offer the greatest choice and quantity of resources for birds, and hence support the most individuals and species. This leads us to our top strategy for developing a home landscape most attractive to birds: to increase the area, diversity, and resource intensity of edge habitats, vertical layers, and mid-successional plant communities. These configurations are the best opportunities in our home landscapes to offer diverse and abundant resources for birds.

If diverse and abundant resources are the ammunition, good fit is the aim. Good fit involves learning about the habitats and plants of your region and neighborhood, as well as which birds you are most likely to attract and their natural preferences. The countryside surrounding your home and the kinds of bird habitats it supports are important in determining the kinds of birds that you will attract.

The following pages of this chapter help you to pinpoint in your own landscape the best places and methods for enriching habitat with plants and other resources attractive to birds.

A WORD ABOUT STYLE

Birds pay little heed to landscape beauty and style. What is of great concern to birds, however, is our human tendency to be excessively neat and orderly. The most effective bird-attracting landscapes are usually quite natural in appearance, with plenty of loose, rough edges—gardens, for example, where leaves are left as mulch, where dying trees and snags are carefully preserved, and where deadfalls and brush piles are allowed to accumulate in out-of-the-way spots.

Avoid using toxic chemicals when gardening for birds. The materials may be directly detrimental to birds, but, even more likely, they may affect the availability of vital insect food. If you want to attract birds, relax. Cultivate an "eat and let eat" attitude, where a few holes in leaves are seen as a positive sign that resources for birds are present.

You enjoy the beauty of flowers, but birds appreciate the nutritious seeds. Choose sunflowers and other daisies to attract small seed-eating birds such as this male American Goldfinch.

Supply birds with safe nesting places to increase the resident bird life in your yard. A hedgerow or groups of dense shrubs may attract sparrows, catbirds, and others, such as the Yellow Warblers shown here.

LANDSCAPE ELEMENTS IMPORTANT TO BIRDS

As you use the following pages to identify how you can enrich your garden as a bird habitat, keep in mind these landscape elements important to birds.

PLANTS: Increase the variety and numbers of plants attractive to birds in your landscape and you are virtually guaranteed more birds that stay longer. Deciding where to work a generous number of plants into your landscape can be a little tricky. Edges between habitats are prime opportunities to offer a dense and diverse assortment of bird-attracting plants. Where woods meet open lawn, for example, is a good spot for a mixed border of shrubs and small trees. Enriching layers in the landscape, such as adding an understory of evergreen shrubs to a deciduous woods, is another way to increase its bird-attracting power. In the pages that follow, we show you many different opportunities for enriching edges and layers with plants.

Plants native to your region are excellent for birds, because they are familiar and accepted as food sources and shelter and nest sites. Native fruits and berries are nutritious, and they ripen on a schedule that coincides with natural needs at nesting and migration time, or during winter months. They are also perfectly sized for birds to eat, unlike some improved varieties or exotic plants whose fruits are unpalatable or too big.

However, some exotic plants (those native to distant regions) also provide birds with food and shelter and should not be dismissed. The lists concluding this chapter will help you choose both exotic and native plants attractive to birds.

WATER: Water is an irresistible lure for nearly all birds. In "Providing Water" (pages 48–57) you will find many specific ways to offer water in your garden. Here we help you decide where in your landscape to do so.

LANDFORM: From the nooks and crannies of rock outcrops to sunny slopes and shady, moist dips, changes in contour are appealing to many birds. If your property is flat, you may want to create slopes or install rocky areas or berms (artificial hillocks). Not only will your land be more interesting, it will attract birds seeking shelter and food.

STRUCTURES: Don't overlook the sides of your house, garage, or shed for habitat enrichment. By growing vines there you can provide birds with food and nest sites. And along with arbors and gazebos, such structures are good places to install nesting shelves.

OPEN SPACE: The spacing between trees and shrubs, the preferred combination of open areas and adjoining thick cover, and the degree of seclusion and protection from wind are all important factors to keep in mind when designing for birds. For the most part, even open spaces should be well-protected from wind and street noise to appeal to birds.

This landscape attracts birds with an abundant cover of trees and shrubs, plus the irresistible draw of water. Notice the variety of vegetation and the mix of open space and shelter, which mimics the edge habitat that many birds find so appealing.

THE IDEAL BIRD GARDEN

This plan (right) may not fit your location exactly, but it illustrates important concepts about what birds find attractive. It provides food, cover, and water in a variety of ways, and it is richly stocked with the plants birds like most (see the lists on pages 30–33).

The property is fortunate to lie at the intersection of two major habitats. To the west are older homes with a lot of mature trees and a forested park beyond. To the north and east are newer homes with shrubs and lawns, with some abandoned farm fields farther away that will eventually be developed for new homes. If it were completely surrounded by forest, this garden might be seen as a large "woodland opening." If it were completely surrounded by open lands, it might be seen as an isolated grove.

In this garden a variety of edge formations are especially pronounced features. The "woodland opening" in the northwest corner is intensified at its edge **(1)** by dense plantings of understory shrubs and small trees resembling a waterside thicket and the addition of a small pool and water garden. Within the wooded area at the far corner **(2)** is a brush pile. About half of the canopy and understory plants are evergreen and half are deciduous. The ground layer under trees and shrubs is a combination of groundcover and leaf mulch. In the more open side of the backyard, the lawn is broken up with an island-bed "oasis" of perennials with a birdbath **(3)**; this "meadow" planting is repeated in the bed at the northeast corner **(4)**. Where one type of vegetation merges into another, such as the intersection of lawn, woodland, and meadow plantings in the peninsula at the top center, is an excellent spot to concentrate resources such as bird feeders **(5)** that are within easy view of the house. In the northeast corner and along the east property line is a "hedgerow" of berry-producing shrubs and seed-producing annuals and perennials **(6)**. This is also a good area for bluebird houses on fence posts. The generous paths on either side of the house **(7)** are mulched. In front, at the "waterside" planting of street trees and thickets of shrubs **(8)**, a small ground pool has been added. The same "waterside" planting is repeated along the drive **(9)**. The house is surrounded with dense foundation shrubs that have been pulled back from important view windows to create secluded yet highly visible areas for feeding stations **(10)**. A large mound planted with groundcover is separated from the lawn with a low rock wall **(11)**. The addition of vines on this stone-faced house **(12)** and small trees at its foundation further emphasize its resemblance to a large outcrop.

This garden illustrates how you can increase the diversity and abundance of bird resources around your home by intensifying edges and layers. The numbered areas in the diagram are described in the accompanying text.

IF YOUR LANDSCAPE IS MOSTLY TREES

Look up to see the brilliant male Scarlet Tanager, a bird that spends most of its time searching for insects in the forest canopy.

Nuthatches, the Brown Creeper, thrushes, and tanagers are a few of the special birds that may visit your woodland garden. Dense cover beneath a canopy of trees is vital to many forest songbirds, whose natural habitat is becoming increasingly scarce or fragmented into smaller pieces due to development. If your woodsy garden is an island in the sea of suburbia, it may offer a haven to some of these displaced birds. If your property adjoins native woodland, it is even more important to keep it as close to its natural state as possible and avoid the effects of habitat destruction.

If you are blessed with a stand of trees, avoid clearing the space between them to have a parklike setting of lawn and trees. In moist forest areas such as the East and Northwest, many shrubs, young trees, and herbaceous plants fill the spaces between the trunks of more mature specimens. Even in areas such as the dry West and the Great Plains, where trees appear isolated in the landscape, they are usually surrounded by high grass, wildflowers, leaf litter, or other natural materials. Again, it is best to take your landscaping lessons from the natural areas around you. Follow the look of the woodsy areas nearby, and birds that dwell there will also be comfortable in your garden.

Transitional zones, such as edges and openings, occur naturally in wooded areas and can be a part of your bird garden as well. Where mature trees abut the open area of a lawn, gardeners often plant borders of shrubs and flowers. The result resembles the thickets of woodland margins and watersides. A pocket of lawn protruding into the shady part of the garden, so that it is partially ringed by trees, resembles a woodland opening. Other low, open areas—the paving of patio and driveway, groundcovers or flowerbeds bordered with trees and shrubs—also function as woodland openings.

Locate especially lush plantings of hedges, shrub borders, and flowers at the margins of your woodland openings to attract birds that appreciate edge habitat, such as hummingbirds, phoebes, titmice, and orioles. These birds appreciate the open flying space of driveways, lawns, and other corridors, which allow them easy access to plants along the edges.

In all bird landscapes, a diversity of plants

A layered garden that includes young trees, shrubs, and other plants beneath taller trees attracts birds of the forest, such as the White-throated Sparrow and thrushes, to the familiar surroundings. In the drier Southwest and plains, where vegetation is more sparse, native grasses or fallen leaves beneath trees are more appropriate and more appealing to native birds.

provides the greatest benefit. Berries and seeds will ripen at various times of the year, a range of nesting materials and nest sites will be available, and a greater variety of insects will be found on the plants.

Keep in mind that a natural woodland is generally free from human traffic, which can disturb the often shy birds of the forest. Let your plantings fill in, and accept a bit of disorder so that birds aren't unnecessarily disturbed by your efforts to keep the garden manicured.

MAKING YOUR WOODLAND LANDSCAPE MORE ATTRACTIVE TO BIRDS

■ **PROVIDE SEVERAL LAYERS** for different kinds of birds by planting clusters of shade-loving small trees, shrubs, and groundcovers under taller trees. Look at natural woodlands around you to get ideas for plant combinations.

■ **LET FALLEN LEAVES LIE** instead of raking them away. Let them nestle around your plantings and settle into a bed of mulch that adds to the soil as well as creating insect-rich areas for ground-dwelling birds to forage.

■ **ADD SPRING WILDFLOWERS** that fade into dormancy after blooming, such as bloodroot, Virginia bluebells, and trillium. They are excellent choices for adding color to shady gardens. When these plants are dormant, the open spaces of leaf litter above their roots provide an important resource for ground-level forest dwellers, such as thrushes.

■ **PLANT NATIVE FERNS,** which grow well beneath trees and in shady areas. Their fronds provide good cover for birds that move about on the forest floor.

■ **LET MOSSES AND MUSHROOMS THRIVE,** two signs that your shade garden is becoming naturally more diverse. Many birds use moss to line their nests.

■ **INCLUDE ABOUT HALF EVERGREEN, HALF DECIDUOUS PLANTS** in your woodland. Conifers and other evergreens provide year-round cover for the birds in your garden, plus food and nest sites. In addition to planting tall evergreens, you can adjust the plants in the understory to provide the benefits of evergreens to birds of lower levels.

■ **PLANT MARGINS OF OPENINGS** already existing in your landscape with dense shrubs, grasses, flowers, and other plants especially attractive to birds. Lawns, patios, walks, the street, and the drive are all candidates.

■ **INCLUDE WATER FEATURES** to entice birds to drink or bathe. To provide choice, locate at least one at the woodland edge right next to shrubby cover and another in an opening well away from cover where predators may hide.

■ **MAINTAIN A BRUSH PILE** by piling sticks, twigs, and branches in an out-of-the-way spot to attract sparrows, towhees, and other birds.

■ **CAREFULLY PRESERVE DEAD TREES.** Snags (large dead branches), standing dead trees, deadfalls (fallen trees), and stumps are excellent bird attractors, thanks to the insects and larvae that burrow into their wood. Snags make sought-after nesting sites for nuthatches, woodpeckers, chickadees, and other cavity-nesting birds. Fallen logs left in place may attract the rare Pileated Woodpecker. To be safe remove dead trees or snags that are weakened at the bottom from root rot.

Features of a Woodland Landscape for Birds

1. A 50-50 mix of evergreen and deciduous trees and shrubs
2. Layered understory of trees, shrubs, groundcovers, and mulch
3. Plantings resemble waterside thickets at edge of lawn and drive
4. Lawns enhanced with pools and water gardens
5. Leaf-mulched paths provide forage for ground-dwelling birds
6. Groundcover of evergreen plants and ephemeral wildflowers
7. Dead tree carefully preserved
8. Brush piles maintained in hidden locations
9. Arbors covered with vines are good sites for nesting shelves
10. Vines on trellises against house provide food and cover

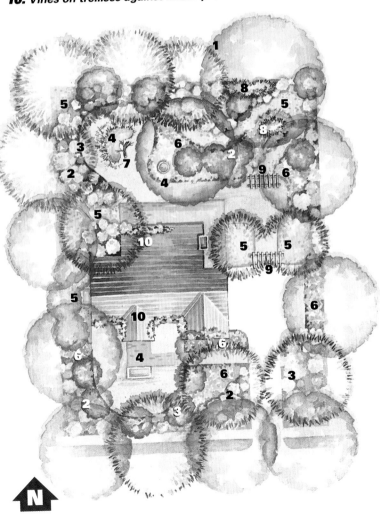

IF YOUR LANDSCAPE IS MOSTLY SHRUBS AND LAWN

Features of an Open-Country Bird Landscape
1. Meadow
2. Small grove of trees, shrubs
3. Brush pile
4. Dead tree
5. Crushed rock
6. Waterfalls over rock wall into bog garden
7. Hedgerow
8. Restricted lawn areas
9. Birdbaths
10. Mulched side-yard paths
11. Grove around house
12. Arbors with vines for nesting

Sunny landscapes with areas of lawn broken up by shrubs, flowers, and fruiting trees are most likely to attract birds of neighboring open country. Such birds include the California Quail, Northern Mockingbird, American Goldfinch, and Song Sparrow. The previous chapter mentions that prominences (groves, oases, and isolated trees) and patches of shrubs mixed with grassy areas form important edges for open-country birds. In many open lawns and gardens, these features are already part of the landscape.

A sunny, open expanse of lawn is often interrupted by an oasis of shrubs and flowers. The house itself is a kind of island, or prominence, and in many gardens its functional resemblance to a rock outcrop is increased by dense foundation plantings of trees, shrubs, and vines. Birds drawn to garden islands include the Red-bellied Woodpecker, Northern Flicker, Black-capped Chickadee, and Song Sparrow. A strip of shrubby vegetation, such as a hedge along a drive,

may be frequented by the Yellow Warbler, Northern Cardinal, Carolina Wren, and Brown Thrasher.

Hummingbirds, which may also visit shade gardens, are attracted to the bright flower plantings of sunny, open gardens. The open space also allows them to freely perform their aerial courtship displays, in which they swing and loop through the air. Flowers also bring in butterflies and other flying insects, which, when combined with open space and nearby perches, will attract phoebes and bluebirds. These birds generally sit quietly until an insect ventures near, then swoop after it and return to the perch until the next meal.

MAKING YOUR OPEN-COUNTRY LANDSCAPE MORE ATTRACTIVE TO BIRDS

■ **INTENSIFY THE PROMINENCE** you already have—the house—by planting a few trees close to it. Also plant foundation shrubs and vines if you don't already have them. (For a list of vines that attract birds, see page 32.)

■ **LEAVE SPACES BETWEEN FOUNDATION PLANTS AND VIEW WINDOWS** to resemble clearings. Such spaces are excellent spots to offer food at feeders. By keeping the areas near windows clear, you can maintain open views to the yard beyond.

■ **OFFER WATER**—it is one of the most important things you can do to attract birds in open-country regions, where water is usually a scarce resource. Try to offer water in several ways, and keep it reliably supplied.

■ **ESTABLISH A SECOND PROMINENCE** away from the house but within view by planting an isolated, fast-growing tree, such as a honey locust, pin oak, or red maple. Even more effective and immediate is planting a small grove of three, five, or seven young trees (odd numbers look best in a grouping). If you already have an isolated tree surrounded by plenty of space, make it more attractive to birds by ringing it with a few younger trees of the same kind, as if they were saplings in a developing grove. (For a list of fast-growing trees to plant in small groves, see page 33.)

■ **CREATE OPENINGS** in large, continuous beds of shrubs by removing some shrubs and replacing them with a grass path and a bed of flowers. Openings in brush and scrub habitats are as important to birds as are openings in woodlands. Rather than solid plantings of shrubs, most birds prefer brushy habitats broken up by grassy patches.

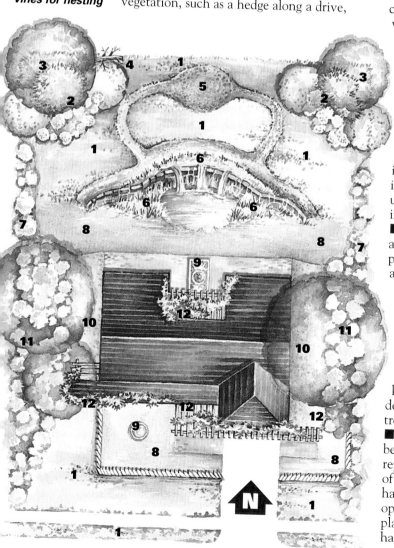

■ **VARY THE HEIGHT, DENSITY, AND FRUITING SEASON OF YOUR SHRUB BEDS** by planting tall shrubs, small fruiting trees, perennials and ornamental grasses, and low groundcovers.

■ **INSTALL A SMALL ARBOR PLANTED WITH VINES** at the garden gate or in a quiet seating area in the yard. A nesting shelf for American Robins is particularly appropriate at such an intimate site. Mourning Doves might nest there too.

■ **PLANT VINES** on trellises and fences too. Flowering vines bloom freely in sunny gardens and are an easy way to add height. Trellised vines also serve as windbreaks. Many flowering vines attract hummingbirds (see lists on pages 31 and 32 for suggestions).

■ **INCREASE VARIETY IN YOUR LAWN** by converting part of it to mixed beds of flowers, shrubs, and fruiting trees. Plant island beds in the center of the lawn, and borders around the perimeter, along the property lines, and next to the drive and paths. Birdbaths and feeders intensify the usefulness of open lawn.

■ **PLANT GENEROUS BEDS OF SHRUBS AND FLOWERS** to increase the allure of your open-country landscape. Or plant trees that in later years will form a large woodland grove with a central clearing. The birds will enjoy the shrubby thicket habitat that small trees provide while you wait for the grove to mature into a canopy.

■ **LEAVE HEDGES UNCLIPPED,** or prune them naturally by selective branch removal rather than shearing. Hedges, which are well-used by many birds, should be informal and

Bold and striking, the Red-headed Woodpecker is common in some areas of open country but absent in other similar spaces. Attract this bird to your open-country garden with a prominent post, a well-stocked bird feeder, and appealing food plants such as corn and grapes.

natural. Restrict pruning to late winter, if possible, after any loose fruit has been eaten and before birds begin nesting in early spring.

■ **LEAVE SPENT FLOWERS** as much as possible in your flowerbed to provide food for birds when the seeds ripen. Plant perennials and annuals that birds favor, especially those whose seed heads are an asset to the fall and winter garden. Native ornamental grasses are excellent choices.

Water dripping into a ground pool, lots of space, and sizable plants for quick cover make this California garden especially attractive to birds of open spaces such as quail and sparrows. Trees and posts are tempting perching places from which thrashers and other visitors can sing or survey their territory.

IF YOU HAVE A SMALL OUTDOOR SPACE

Containers and trellises make a garden of hummingbird delights possible even in a small space. Trellises of trumpet honeysuckle (Lonicera sempervirens) and trumpet vine (Campsis radicans), and pots filled with red salvias (Salvia splendens, S. coccinea) signal the birds with zingy red and orange-red flowers.

A small lawn or garden can be a haven in an urban neighborhood, a welcome pocket of life to birds in a habitat that, to them, resembles a series of barren, rocky canyons. Even foliage spilling out of a window box or flowers dangling from a hanging pot of fuchsia outside a window can attract passing birds and keep them coming back if you offer other inducements. A wide variety of wildlife braves the concrete of our cities. You're fortunate if you live near a park or greenbelt, but it's not necessary for attracting birds. They will seek you out if you supply food, water, and protective cover.

CREATING A SMALL-SCALE HAVEN FOR BIRDS

■ **PROVIDE VARIETY.** Establish a perimeter of small trees around a patch of lawn. In one corner install a tiny pool backed by dwarf shrubs, small trees, and flowers. (For lists of small plants attractive to birds, see page 31.)
■ **DECORATE YOUR DECK OR A BALCONY WITH PLANTER BOXES** of flowers and deciduous and evergreen shrubs. To passing birds this habitat will resemble a ledge on a cliff that has caught a bit of soil, seeds, and water. A small tree in a tub increases the

effect of the mini-oasis. Although the greenery you grow will catch birds' attention, you will have to offer supplemental food and water to keep them returning. Many birdbaths and feeders fit nicely on terraces and look attractive too.
■ **PROVIDE WATER.** Small fountains sold for home decor nestle nicely in a courtyard or on a balcony, where the sound of running water will be a powerful attractant to birds. Use a heavy-duty outside electrical cord to power the pump, or invest in a solar-powered one.
■ **EXPERIMENT WITH CONTAINER PLANTS,** such as dwarf sunflowers for goldfinches, or prairie grasses and coneflowers (*Echinacea purpurea* and *Ratibida* spp.) for native sparrows.
■ **PLANT DENSELY** to fit in more flowers: In a wooden half-barrel planter, you can squeeze in three stout sunflowers, a dozen cosmos, and an edging of dwarf or creeping zinnia—all good birdseed flowers for finches, cardinals, and other seedeaters.
■ **HANG A WINDOW BOX** to offer a green spot to attract passing birds and blooms for hummingbirds to feed on. Window-mounted bird feeders, hummingbird feeders, and a twelve-inch pan of water on the sill will welcome birds and keep them coming back.

FOOD GARDENS AND BIRDS

Few bird species are really destructive. Many feed primarily on insects; in fact, birds are one of nature's most effective ways of controlling pests. During spring and summer—the times when your garden is most vulnerable to insect attack—most birds are great aids in the garden, gleaning caterpillars, squash bugs, and other pests from plants.

However, if you are serious about raising vegetables, fruits, and berries, you'll probably want to protect your crops. Some birds love the fruits we grow in gardens. Teaching them to come to your garden is an open invitation to raid your orchard and berry patch.

PROTECTING FOOD GARDENS FROM BIRDS

■ **PROTECT FRUIT TREES AND BUSHES WITH BIRD NETTING.** Available at most nurseries, home and garden centers, and hardware stores, bird netting is the most practical and effective way to protect trees and shrubs. Birds often eat the flowers of fruit trees, reducing the yield of fruit, so put up the nets as soon as flowers start to open.

To protect large trees, throw the netting over the top of the tree and cover the foliage completely. Fasten the netting to the trunk to prevent birds from getting trapped beneath it. Birds may eat the fruit they can reach through the netting, but the rest will be protected.

To protect small fruit trees and berry bushes, build a frame of 2×2s around the plants and cover the frame with bird netting.

■ **WRAP APPLES, PEARS, AND OTHER FRUITS IN PAPER OR CHEESECLOTH BAGS.** Protect grapes by enclosing each developing cluster as soon as the fruit sets. Protect corn in the same way, after the ears are pollinated. Don't use plastic bags; heat and moisture build up inside them.

■ **HANG SHINY OBJECTS THAT FLAP IN THE WIND,** such as aluminum pie plates or strips of aluminum foil. This may work for a while. Or make a framework of stakes on both sides of a row of fruits or vegetables and tie string between the stakes in a crisscross pattern. Some birds may avoid flying between the strings. The strings also make good supports from which to hang shiny foil.

■ **PLACE PLASTIC NETTING OR SPUN-FIBER FLOATING ROW COVERS OVER LARGE SEEDBEDS.** Remove the netting soon after the seeds sprout, before the plants get too big. Seed-eating birds, such as the House Sparrow, Common Grackle, and House Finch, find newly planted seeds a tasty snack.

■ **PLACE A CAGE OF WIRE MESH OVER SMALL BEDS FRESHLY PLANTED WITH SEED.** Leave the cage in place until the plants develop several sets of mature leaves. Cages about 10×10×24 inches are self-supporting; reinforce larger ones with heavy wire.

Drape or cage blueberry bushes, cherry trees, strawberry beds, and other fruit crops with lightweight plastic netting to keep birds from eating the fruit before you do. Netting or spun-fiber row cover material also protect newly planted garden beds from birds that might eat seeds or seedlings.

HUMMINGBIRDS IN THE GARDEN

Tempt amazing, beautiful hummingbirds to your garden with red tubular flowers. This male Ruby-throated Hummingbird sips from Indian paintbrush (Castilleja spp.). For a list of other flowers that attract hummingbirds, see page 31.

Their shining jewel tones and unique habits make hummingbirds among the most fascinating birds you can attract to your landscape. Their iridescent plumage comes in many hues—fiery red, glowing ruby, deep violet, metallic greens and blues, shimmering bronze, gold, and yellow. The colors change with the bird's every movement and each shift of the light.

Everything about these tiny birds is interesting. With more than 320 species, they are one of the largest bird families, yet they occur only in the Americas. Most species are concentrated in equatorial South America; only 16 species breed north of the Mexican border, and most of those are not widespread. The Anna's, Costa's, Ruby-throated, and Rufous Hummingbirds—four of the most common species in the United States—are described in the "Gallery of Birds" beginning on page 66. In the Rocky Mountains, the Broad-tailed Hummingbird is the common nesting species. The plumage of many hummingbirds is basically green (although the Rufous Hummingbird has a rich reddish back); it's the vivid colors of the throat feathers (gorget) that distinguish one species from another. When not in sun or bright light, the iridescent feathers appear dull or dark.

Despite their minute size, hummingbirds are extremely strong fliers. The Rufous Hummingbird is only about 3½ inches long and it weighs a mere ⅑ ounce, yet it breeds as far north as southern Alaska and winters in Mexico—a migration of more than 2,000 miles. This migration takes place over several weeks, or even months, as the birds follow the blooming season of their favorite flowers. The Ruby-throated Hummingbird is even smaller

(about 3¼ inches and ⅒ ounce) than the Rufous, but it migrates from as far north as southern Canada to as far south as Panama. Many Ruby-throated Hummingbirds cross the Gulf of Mexico—a nonstop flight of 500 miles. In preparation for its long trek, the hummingbird stores up fat, increasing its body weight by as much as 50 percent.

Even when they're not migrating, hummingbirds need to eat relatively huge quantities of food to fuel their rapid metabolism. In fact, ounce for ounce, hummingbirds require more calories than any other warm-blooded animal (except possibly shrews). The calories are necessary to maintain their body temperature of about 105 degrees F and to fuel their extremely rapid movement. In forward flight a hummingbird may beat its wings 75 times per second. No wonder we perceive the creature as a blur.

In flight, hummingbirds are uniquely adapted to gather nectar from their favorite flowers. Not only can they hover motionless before a flower, they can dart backward, up, down, and in any other direction so quickly that they seem to vanish. Many species cannot walk at all. To shift positions on a branch or adjust their bodies on the nest, they simply rise in the air an inch or two and alight in a new position.

FEEDING

Hummingbirds have two major sources of food: flower nectar and the protein from small insects and spiders. The tiny birds also frequently visit the holes that sapsuckers make in trees to drink the sweet sap and to snap up the insects that are also drawn by the sap. Although hummingbirds visit nectar-bearing flowers of all colors, they are most drawn to bright red, pink, and orange tubular flowers. The most important thing you can do to attract these birds is to plant flowering annuals, perennials, shrubs, and trees.

These birds will come eagerly to special feeders stocked with sugar water. The advantage of feeders is that they bring the birds where you want them—close to the house or other places where they can be easily observed. Several models of hummingbird feeders are available. Bright red plastic flowers will guide the birds on their initial visits, although they will soon learn to seek out their rich food even if the location or appearance of the feeder is changed. Start with a small feeder and add more or a larger model when traffic increases.

The formula for hummingbird food is simple: about 1 part white granulated sugar to 4 parts water. Boil the water, add the sugar, stir until it dissolves thoroughly, and let cool. Store any unused solution in the refrigerator.

Fill the feeders daily. Every four or five days, take them down and rinse thoroughly with hot water to which a little vinegar has been added; this prevents mold from becoming established. Scrub the feeders with a baby-bottle brush, and rinse thoroughly before refilling them.

Don't use honey solution in the feeders; it is a likely medium for the growth of a fungus that can infect the tongues of hummingbirds. And don't add red food coloring to the sugar solution, although the color is attractive. Instead, wrap the feeder with red plastic ribbon or red tape.

The sweet, sticky sugar-water solution is also attractive to insects—including ants, flies, bees, and wasps. If ants find their way to the feeder, apply a generous smear of vegetable oil or petroleum jelly on the wire from which the feeder hangs. This should prevent the ants from reaching the food. To discourage flying insects, try putting petroleum jelly around the feeder openings. Plastic grates called bee guards, which snap over feeder openings, also deter flying insects.

A temporary means of insect control is spraying the feeder with a fine mist from a hose or sprinkler: Insects are discouraged by the water, and any sugar solution that has been spilled on the outside of the feeder will be washed away. And hummingbirds love to flit in and out of the spray.

Many birds besides hummingbirds are attracted to these feeders—including some sparrows, chickadees, finches, nuthatches, orioles, and woodpeckers. These birds usually visit hummingbird feeders that have perches. To accommodate all your sugar-water drinkers, add a perchless feeder for hummingbirds, which can hover to feed.

NESTING

The nests of hummingbirds are so tiny—about the diameter of a half-dollar—and so well-camouflaged that they are seldom noticed. In most cases the male's responsibility ends when the eggs are fertilized. The female constructs her nest primarily of plant down bound with spiderwebs and saliva. The outside of the nest is camouflaged with bits of moss and lichen, so that it is virtually indistinguishable from the branch to which it is attached. Each egg—there are usually two of them—is the size of a small bean. The mother incubates the eggs, without help from the male, for 15 to 19 days, depending on the species.

Newly hatched hummingbirds are almost completely featherless. The mother feeds them for about 25 days, by which time they leave the nest and begin to fend for themselves. Some hummingbirds raise two or even three broods each breeding season.

PLANTING FOR HUMMINGBIRDS

Not only do flowers provide nectar, they also attract the tiny insects and spiders that are an important part of the hummingbird's diet. In the wild these birds prefer meadows, lowland forest edges, and woodland openings, especially near running water, although some species also frequent deserts. To maximize the effect of plantings in your garden, plant flowers in clusters rather than scattering them around. Plant trumpet vines or noninvasive, native honeysuckle on a trellis at the back of the garden, with groups of tall flowers in front of it. An island of flowers or shrubbery in an expanse of lawn is also welcoming to hummingbirds. Even a window box or container plant with a mass of blooms is likely to attract a tiny guest. Because hummingbirds can become territorial about food sources, include tempting red flowers in several plantings so that guests have more than one location to visit.

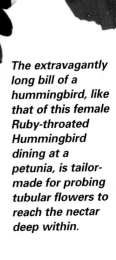

The extravagantly long bill of a hummingbird, like that of this female Ruby-throated Hummingbird dining at a petunia, is tailor-made for probing tubular flowers to reach the nectar deep within.

A male Anna's Hummingbird drinks from a sugar-water feeder, one of the best aids for bringing hummingbirds to your garden. To attract hummingbirds to a new feeder quickly, choose one that is accented with red, a color that indicates a potential nectar source.

PLANTS FOR THE BIRD GARDEN

I n this section you will find our top recommendations for flowers, shrubs, trees, and vines that are highly attractive to birds. Many of these plants are native to North America, but some are highly rated garden plants from other places throughout the world. All are attractive to birds, but they are also garden-worthy plants that are both beautiful and easy to grow. Plants are arranged alphabetically by common name, with the botanical name in parentheses so you can look up a plant in garden books to get information about growing it. To find out which plants grow best in your area and will best fill your specific needs, see Ortho's series of gardening books, available wherever quality books are sold.

Ripe seeds of purple coneflower (Echinacea purpurea) bring the American Goldfinch to the garden. This long-blooming perennial, also a butterfly favorite, holds mature seed heads, fresh blossoms, and buds all at the same time.

ANNUALS FOR SEEDS

Ageratum (*Ageratum* spp.)
Amaranth (*Amaranthus* spp.)
Bachelor's button (*Centaurea cyanus*)
Basket flower (*Centauria americana*)
Big quaking grass (*Briza maxima*)
Blanket flower (*Gaillardia pulchella*)
Blessed thistle (*Cnicus benedictus*)
California poppy (*Eschscholzia californica*)
Cockscomb (*Celosia* spp.)
Coreopsis (*Coreopsis* spp.)
Corn (*Zea mays*)
Cosmos (*Cosmos* spp.)
Dusty miller (*Centaurea cineraria*)
Forget-me-not (*Myosotis* spp.)
Garden balsam (*Impatiens balsamina*)
Love grass (*Eragrostis tef*)
Love-in-a-mist (*Nigella damascena*)
Lupine (*Lupinus* spp.)
Marigold (*Tagetes* spp.)
Mexican sunflower (*Tithonia rotundifolia*)
Milo (*Sorghum bicolor*)
Moss rose (*Portulaca grandiflora*)
Phlox, annual (*Phlox drummondii*)
Plains bristlegrass (*Setaria macrostachya*)
Poppy (*Papaver*, all annual spp.)
Pot marigold (*Calendula officinalis*)
Sea lavender (*Limonium* spp.)
Snapdragon (*Antirrhinum* spp.)
Sunflower (*Helianthus annuus, H. debilis*)
Sweet alyssum (*Lobularia maritima*)
Tickseed (*Bidens* spp.)
Witch grass (*Panicum capillare*)
Zinnia (*Zinnia* spp.)

PERENNIALS FOR SEEDS

Anise hyssop (*Agastache foeniculum*)
Aster (*Aster* spp.)
Black-eyed Susan (*Rudbeckia fulgida*)
Blazing star (*Liatris* spp.)
Bluestem, big (*Andropogon gerardii*)
Bluestem, little (*Schizachyrium scoparium*)
Bulbous oatgrass (*Arrhenatherum elatius* var. *bulbosum*)
Coneflower (*Echinacea* spp.)
Coreopsis (*Coreopsis* spp.)
Deer tongue grass (*Panicum clandestinum*)
Desert marigold (*Baileya multiradiata*)
False indigo (*Baptisia* spp.)
Feather grass (*Stipa* spp.)
Globe thistle (*Echinops* spp.)
Gloriosa daisy (*Rudbeckia hirta*)
Goldenrod (*Solidago* spp.)
Indian grass (*Sorghastrum nutans*)
Mexican hat (*Ratibida* spp.)
Mullein (*Verbascum* spp.)
Northern sea oats (*Chasmanthium latifolium*)
Pinks (*Dianthus* spp.)
Pokeweed (*Phytolacca americana*)
Queen Anne's lace (*Daucus carota*)
Scabiosa (*Scabiosa caucasica*)
Sedge (*Carex* spp.)
Smartweed (*Polygonum* spp.)
Statice (*Limonium* spp.)
Sunflower (*Helianthus maximilianii, H. grosse-serratus,* and other perennial spp.)
Switch grass (*Panicum virgatum*)
Tufted hair grass (*Deschampsia caespitosa*)

FLOWERS ATTRACTIVE TO HUMMINGBIRDS

ANNUALS
Begonia (*Begonia* spp.)
Flowering tobacco (*Nicotiana* spp.)
Four-o-clock (*Mirabilis* spp.)
Garden balsam (*Impatiens balsamina*)
Geranium (*Pelargonium* spp.)
Larkspur (*Consolida ambigua*)
Mexican sunflower (*Tithonia rotundifolia*)
Nasturtium (*Tropaeolum majus*)
Parrot's beak (*Lotus berthelotii*)
Petunia (*Petunia* spp.)
Phlox, annual (*Phlox drummondii*)
Salvia; sage (*Salvia*, all annual spp.)
Scarlet runner bean (*Phaseolus coccineus*)
Spider flower (*Cleome* spp.)
Zinnia (*Zinnia* spp.)

PERENNIALS
Aloe (*Aloe* spp.)
Bee balm (*Monarda* spp.)
California fuchsia (*Epilobium* spp.)
Canna (*Canna* spp.)
Cardinal flower (*Lobelia cardinalis*)
Columbine (*Aquilegia* spp.)
Coral bells (*Heuchera sanguinea*)
Delphinium (*Delphinium* spp.)
Fire pink (*Silene virginica*)
Gilia (*Ipomopsis* spp.)
Great blue lobelia (*Lobelia siphilitica*)
Hibiscus (*Hibiscus* spp.)
Hollyhock (*Alcea rosea*)
Maltese cross (*Lychnis chalcedonica*)
Monkey flower (*Mimulus* spp.)
Paintbrush (*Castilleja* spp.)
Penstemon (*Penstemon* spp.)
Red hot poker (*Kniphofia* spp.)
Salvia (*Salvia*, all perennial spp.)

SMALL TREES, SHRUBS, AND VINES
Agave (*Agave* spp.)
Bottlebrush (*Callistemon* spp.)
Butterfly bush (*Buddleia* spp.)
Canary creeper (*Tropaeolum peregrinum*)
Cape honeysuckle (*Tecomaria capensis*)
Citrus (*Citrus* spp.)
Coral bean (*Erythrina* spp.)
Cross vine (*Bignonia capreolata*)
Currant (*Ribes* spp.)
Fuchsia (*Fuchsia* spp.)
Honeysuckle (*Lonicera*, native spp.)
Manzanita (*Arctostaphylos* spp.)
Ocotillo (*Fouquieria splendens*)
Red buckeye (*Aesculus pavia*)
Trumpet creeper (*Campsis* spp.)
Weigela (*Weigela* spp.)

PLANTS FOR SMALL PLACES

SMALL TREES
Crabapple (*Malus* spp.)
Dogwood (*Cornus* spp.)
Fringe tree (*Chionanthus* spp.)
Hawthorn (*Crataegus* spp.)
Holly (*Ilex* spp.)
Hornbeam (*Carpinus* spp.)
Mountain ash (*Sorbus* spp.)
Plum; cherry (*Prunus* spp.)
Sassafras (*Sassafras albidum*)
Serviceberry (*Amelanchier* spp.)

SHRUBS
American cranberrybush viburnum
    (*Viburnum trilobum* 'Compactum')
Blueberry (*Vaccinium*, dwarf varieties)
Box huckleberry (*Gaylussacia* spp.)
Holly (*Ilex* spp.)
Juniper (*Juniperus* spp.)
Mugo pine (*Pinus mugo* 'Compacta')
Pacific serviceberry (*Amelanchier florida*)
Palmetto (*Sabal minor*)
Salal (*Gaultheria shallon*)
Spicebush (*Lindera benzoin*)
Vernal witch hazel (*Hamamelis vernalis*)
Yew (*Taxus* spp.)

Hawthorn berries attract a male Northern Cardinal in winter.

PLANTS FOR THE BIRD GARDEN
continued

The abundant fruit clusters of red elderberry (Sambucus pubens) provide a feast for many birds, including this male Rose-breasted Grosbeak.

EVERGREEN TREES AND SHRUBS FOR SHELTER, SEEDS, AND FRUITS

American holly (*Ilex opaca*)
Bayberry (*Myrica pensylvanica, M. californica, M. cerifera*)
Douglas fir (*Pseudotsuga menziesii*)
Fir (*Abies* spp.)
Grapeholly (*Mahonia* spp.)
Hemlock (*Tsuga* spp.)
Japanese yew (*Taxus cuspidata*)
Juniper (*Juniperus* spp.)
Pine (*Pinus* spp.)
Salal (*Gaultheria shallon*)
Southern magnolia (*Magnolia grandiflora*)
Spruce (*Picea* spp.)
Yew (*Taxus* spp.)

SHRUBS FOR HEDGES

Arrowwood viburnum (*Viburnum dentatum*)
Bayberry (*Myrica pensylvanica, M. californica, M. cerifera*)
Blackberry; raspberry; bramble (*Rubus* spp.)
Boxleaf honeysuckle (*Lonicera nitida*)
Cherry laurel (*Prunus laurocerasus*)
Cotoneaster (*Cotoneaster* spp.)
Elder (*Sambucus* spp.)
Firethorn (*Pyracantha* spp.)
Fragrant sumac (*Rhus aromatica*)
Gray dogwood (*Cornus racemosa*)
Red-osier dogwood (*Cornus stolonifera*)
Winterberry (*Ilex verticillata*)
Yaupon (*Ilex vomitoria*)

SMALL, FRUITING TREES AND SHRUBS FOR FULL SUN

SMALL TREES
American holly (*Ilex opaca*)
Apple (*Malus,* any cultivar)
Carolina cherry laurel (*Prunus caroliniana*)
Dogwood (*Cornus* spp.)
　Cornelian cherry (*C. mas*)
　Flowering dogwood (*C. florida*)
Hackberry; sugarberry (*Celtis* spp.)
Hawthorn (*Crataegus* spp.)
Mountain ash (*Sorbus* spp.)
Mulberry (*Morus* spp.)
Orange (*Citrus sinensis*)
Plum; cherry (*Prunus* spp.)
Serviceberry (*Amelanchier* spp.)

SHRUBS
Bayberry, wax myrtle (*Myrica* spp.)
Beach plum (*Prunus maritima*)
Beautyberry (*Callicarpa* spp.)
Blackberry; raspberry; bramble (*Rubus* spp.)
Blueberry (*Vaccinium* spp.)
Buffaloberry (*Shepherdia argentea*)
Chokeberry (*Aronia* spp.)
Cotoneaster (*Cotoneaster* spp.)
Currant (*Ribes* spp.)
Elder (*Sambucus* spp.)
Firethorn (*Pyracantha* spp.)
Grapeholly (*Mahonia* spp.)
Holly (*Ilex* spp.)
　Chinese holly (*I. cornuta*)
　Foster's holly (*I. × attenuata* 'Fosteri')
　Possumhaw (*I. decidua*)
　Winterberry (*I. verticillata*)
Red-osier dogwood (*Cornus stolonifera*)
Snowberry (*Symphoricarpos* spp.)
Spicebush (*Lindera benzoin*)
Sumac (*Rhus* spp.)
Viburnum (*Viburnum* spp.)
　American cranberrybush viburnum (*V. trilobum*)
　Arrowwood viburnum (*V. dentatum*)
Western sandcherry (*Prunus besseyi*)

VINES

American bittersweet (*Celastrus scandens*)
Cross vine (*Bignonia capreolata*)
Grape (*Vitis* spp.)
Honeysuckle (*Lonicera* spp.)
　Everblooming honeysuckle (*L. × heckrottii*)
　Trumpet honeysuckle (*L. sempervirens*)
Virginia creeper (*Parthenocissus quinquefolia*)

SHADE-TOLERANT TREES AND SHRUBS FOR WOODLAND UNDERSTORY

SMALL TREES

American hornbeam (*Carpinus caroliniana*)
American persimmon (*Diospyros virginiana*)
Birch (*Betula* spp.)
Dogwood (*Cornus* spp.)
   Cornelian cherry (*C. mas*)
   Flowering dogwood (*C. florida*)
   Pagoda dogwood (*C. alternifolia*)
Hawthorn (*Crataegus* spp.)
Hemlock (*Tsuga* spp.)
Holly (*Ilex* spp.)
   American holly (*I. opaca*)
   Nellie Stevens holly (*I.* × 'Nellie R. Stevens')
Japanese maple (*Acer palmatum*)
Red buckeye (*Aesculus pavia*)
Redbud (*Cercis* spp.)
Serviceberry (*Amelanchier* spp.)
   Allegheny serviceberry (*A. laevis*)
   Apple serviceberry (*A.* × *grandiflora*)
   Downy serviceberry (*A. arborea*)

SHRUBS

Blackberry; raspberry; bramble (*Rubus* spp.)
Box huckleberry (*Gaylussacia* spp.)
Cotoneaster (*Cotoneaster* spp.)
Currant (*Ribes* spp.)
Dogwood (*Cornus* spp.)
   Blood-twig dogwood (*C. sanguinea*)
   Gray dogwood (*C. racemosa*)
   Red-osier dogwood (*C. stolonifera*)
   Silky dogwood (*C. amomum*)
   Tatarian dogwood (*C. alba*)
Elder (*Sambucus* spp.)
Fragrant sumac (*Rhus aromatica*)
Grapeholly (*Mahonia* spp.)
Holly (*Ilex* spp.)
   Common winterberry (*I. verticillata*)
   Possumhaw (*I. decidua*)
Huckleberry (*Vaccinium* spp.)
Manzanita (*Arctostaphylos* spp.)
Salal (*Gaultheria shallon*)
Salmonberry (*Rubus spectabilis*)
Serviceberry (*Amelanchier* spp.)
   Pacific serviceberry (*A. florida*)
   Running serviceberry (*A. stolonifera*)
Snowberry (*Symphoricarpos* spp.)
Spicebush (*Lindera benzoin*)
Thimbleberry (*Rubus parviflorus*)
Viburnum (*Viburnum* spp.)
   American cranberrybush viburnum (*V. trilobum*)
   Arrowwood viburnum (*V. dentatum*)
   Blackhaw viburnum (*V. lantana*)
   Hobblebush (*V. alnifolium*)
Yew (*Taxus* spp.)

SHADE-TOLERANT GROUNDCOVERS FOR WOODLAND UNDERSTORY

Bearberry (*Arctostaphylos uva-ursi*)
Bearberry cotoneaster (*Cotoneaster dammeri*)
Box huckleberry (*Gaylussacia* spp.)
Bunchberry (*Cornus canadensis*)
Carpet bugle (*Ajuga reptans*)
Creeping cotoneaster (*Cotoneaster adpressus*)
Creeping mahonia (*Mahonia repens*)
Creeping salmonberry (*Rubus pentalobus* 'Emerald Carpet')
Evergreen currant (*Ribes viburnifolium*)
Lilyturf (*Liriope* spp.)
Lingonberry (*Vaccinium vitis-idaea* var. *minus*)
Partridge berry (*Mitchella repens*)
Rockspray cotoneaster (*Cotoneaster horizontalis*)
Running serviceberry (*Amelanchier stolonifera*)
Salal (*Gaultheria shallon*)
Sedge (*Carex* spp.)
Solomon's seal (*Polygonatum* spp.)
Strawberry (*Fragaria* spp.)
Virginia creeper (*Parthenocissus quinquefolia*)
Wintergreen (*Gaultheria procumbens*)

FAST-GROWING TREES FOR SMALL GROVES

Alder (*Alnus* spp.)
Birch (*Betula* spp.)
Black gum (*Nyssa sylvatica*)
Eastern white pine (*Pinus strobus*)
Green ash (*Fraxinus pennsylvanica*)
Hackberry; sugarberry (*Celtis* spp.)
Honey locust (*Gleditsia triacanthos*)
Pin oak (*Q. palustris*)
Poplar; aspen (*Populus* spp.)
Redbud (*Cercis* spp.)
Red maple (*Acer rubrum*)
Staghorn sumac (*Rhus typhina*)
Sweet gum (*Liquidambar styraciflua*)
Tulip tree (*Liriodendron tulipifera*)
Willow oak (*Q. phellos*)

A male American Goldfinch in winter plumage plucks seeds of blazing star (Liatris spp.)

A mockingbird may become aggressively territorial, vigorously chasing away competitors, when it discovers a good food source such as this chokeberry (Aronia arbutifolia).

PROVIDING FOOD

Put up a feeder, and they will come—it's that simple. Be sure to place the feeder where you will have a good view of it.

The secret to successful bird feeding is providing the kind of food that each bird prefers and making it easy for birds to find and eat.

Plants provide food, shelter, and familiar habitat and are essential for attracting birds to your yard. But supplemental feeding stations concentrate large numbers of birds where you can see and appreciate them. A survey by the U.S. Department of the Interior reports that approximately 57 million people in the United States feed wild birds. Three million people feed birds in Canada. The only outdoor hobby that is more popular in North America is gardening. People of all ages are fascinated by watching birds at feeders. A bird feeding hobby has great appeal to those who are housebound. For birds, feeders are a reliable food source that can be counted on regardless of the weather.

Many people begin feeding birds as soon as cool weather sets in during the fall, but the crucial times for feeder birds are winter and early spring, when natural food is scarce.

YEAR-ROUND FEEDING

If the motive for feeding birds is largely to derive satisfaction and entertainment, conduct a year-round feeding program. The warm months bring different birds to the feeder as migratory summer residents return from their southern ranges and winter visitors depart for their breeding places farther north.

Birds tend to scatter at nesting time, becoming more territorial and less social. Instead of a dozen cardinals, only one or two breeding pairs may gather at the feeder, along with other summer residents such as titmice, chickadees, woodpeckers, nuthatches, and finches. In many cases parents bring their offspring to the feeders. Following the example of their parents, young birds learn to gather their own food. Even after they have mastered this art, they continue to demand morsels, crouching before a parent with wings quivering and mouths gaping.

Summer also offers the opportunity to feed hummingbirds, which will visit sugar-water feeders from spring into fall in most parts of the country. In warm areas several hummingbird species are year-round visitors. For hummingbirds that haven't migrated farther southward, it is a hardship not to have the artificial nectar that replaces flower nectar as winter sets in.

Many people discover that attendance at bird feeders is at its lowest in early autumn, largely because fruits, berries, and seeds are plentiful at this time of year and insects and other small invertebrates are numerous. Nevertheless, chickadees and other permanent residents usually continue daily visits to the feeder, advertising the availability of food for other birds.

BIRD FOODS

The mainstays of any bird-feeding program are seeds, grains, nutmeats, and fats in the form of suet and suet mixes. Add bakery products, fruit, and sugar water, and you will satisfy the tastes and needs of many visitors.

One frequently overlooked resource is grit. Birds have no teeth and depend upon hard particles (grit) in their gizzards to grind up whatever passes into their digestive systems. Grit is especially welcome in areas where snow covers the natural supply. One common type of grit, available in garden centers and feed stores, is composed of ground oyster shell. Seashore sand containing fine particles of quartz is another type. Crushed eggshell is a form of grit that supplies birds with calcium and is particularly popular with the Purple Martin. Broadcast the shell on the ground below martin colonies during their nesting season. For other birds, place grit in small containers away from feeders to prevent it from being contaminated by bird droppings.

All oriole species are attracted to fruit and nectar feeders. This male Baltimore Oriole eagerly eats the sweet pulp of an orange, cut in half for easy access.

WHEN YOU CAN'T BE THERE

Birds may be hard-pressed to find food if your feeders are empty during your midwinter vacation. Researchers in rural Wisconsin, using leg bands to identify Black-capped Chickadees and chart their survival, discovered that chickadees in winter obtain less than 25 percent of their food from feeders. Shutting down a feeder during a normal or mild winter had no harmful effects on the patrons, but during a severe winter, that feeder food made a big difference. During harsh winters only 37 percent of those without feeders survived, while 69 percent of the birds that went to feeders did so. To play it safe when you leave, make long-lasting food such as suet available or ask a neighbor to fill your feeder. If neighbors are feeding birds, your birds will have an alternate source of food should your feeders be emptied while you're away.

SEEDS AND GRAINS

Tube feeders filled with niger or sunflower seed are readily used by the American Goldfinch and other finches as well as the Pine Siskin. Waste is minimal with this type of feeder, and seeds are protected from wet weather.

Many excellent birdseed mixtures are available at garden centers, nurseries, and bird-feeding specialty shops, as well as through the mail. Some commercial mixes, however, contain a substantial amount of inexpensive seed that the birds at your feeder are likely to ignore. You may find it more satisfying to offer only one type of seed or make your own mix from bulk seed. This allows you to tailor what you offer to attract the birds you want to attract and discourage those you do not want to attract.

One way to make your own mix is by using a homemade testing tray composed of separate compartments, one for each kind of seed. Label each compartment with the kind of seed it contains, place the tray at your feeding station, and keep a careful record at the end of each day of the amount of each type eaten. Two to three weeks of testing will give you an idea of the relative proportions for a seed mixture that the birds in your area prefer. Because preferences and bird populations change, you may want to continue testing throughout the season.

SUNFLOWER SEED

Once Northern Cardinals sample safflower seed, it quickly becomes a favorite. Game birds eat milo, but most other birds scorn it. Many popular feeder birds eat striped sunflower seed. Finches such as the Pine Siskin favor tiny niger seed, especially when offered in hanging feeders.

Sunflower seed has always been used for feeding cage and wild birds. An oil-rich variety called black-oil sunflower seed was introduced around 1980. Developed especially for wild bird feeding, it has become the most popular seed or grain for this purpose. A survey by Project FeederWatch (see page 92)

established that black-oil sunflower seed was preferred by birds over all other types of sunflower seed. Compared to striped sunflower seed, black-oil sunflower seed has more meat and less hull per seed and is easier for birds to open. Moreover, the black-oil seed, with its high oil content, is richer in protein, fats, vitamins, and minerals. Among those who feed birds, black-oil sunflower seed is two to three times as popular as striped sunflower seed.

For those who do not want to be bothered with sunflower hulls that accumulate below feeders, here is an easy solution: Buy shelled sunflower hearts. Although they are more expensive and have a shorter shelf life than unshelled seed, sunflower hearts are quickly eaten by birds and leave no debris.

Jays and squirrels often bury sunflower seed for later use. As the forgotten seeds sprout, they may become a nuisance in your garden. Using hulled seeds prevents this problem as they will not sprout.

Sunflower seed is primarily a food for seedeaters such as grosbeaks and cardinals, as well as woodpeckers, chickadees, titmice, nuthatches, and jays. Most of these birds prefer to be served food in elevated feeders. An exception is the Northern Cardinal, which will eat at elevated feeders if they have an adequate place to perch. Squirrels and other ground feeders quickly devour sunflower seed from open feeders, so offer it at hopper and tube feeders shielded from squirrels.

Sunflower seed can be offered year-round. It keeps well but, like other seed having a high oil content, tends to become rancid in hot weather. Also, a grain moth (*Sitotroga cerealella*) may infest seed kept too long in storage. Store sunflower seed, as well as other types of seed and grain, in a container with a tight lid and keep it in a cool, dry place— preferably outside of your house. For lengths of time that various bird foods can be safely stored, see the chart on page 39.

Safflower Milo Striped sunflower Niger

SAFFLOWER SEED

Safflower seed is an oil-rich seed used primarily in cooking oil. A native of India, safflower is now being grown in drier parts of the West. Only recently has its virtue as a bird food been discovered: The tough-coated seeds are not eaten by many unwelcome guests but are eaten by birds that most people like. Many preferred birds—the seedeaters as well as chickadees, titmice, and nuthatches—can crack open the hard seed coats with their bills. The Mourning Dove solves the problem by swallowing the seeds whole. Many unpopular birds—the European Starling, Common Grackle, Brown-headed Cowbird, and Red-winged Blackbird, for example—with their differently shaped bills, are unable to crack open the seeds and do not swallow them. They try for a while but soon give up. Squirrels are unpredictable in their reaction to safflower seed. Sometimes they eat it, sometimes they don't.

When safflower seed is first offered at a feeder, birds are usually slow to accept it. But if it is mixed with sunflower seed, birds soon catch on. The Northern Cardinal is one of the first birds to recognize safflower seed as a food. Offer it in tube or hopper feeders. Seeds that fall to the ground are readily consumed by Northern Cardinals and Mourning Doves.

Store safflower seed in the same way as sunflower seed. Safflower seed, with its hard coat, keeps well. It can be used year-round and is regarded by many as one of the best seeds to use in summer. Thanks to its appeal to particular birds, it is becoming more and more popular with those who feed birds.

NIGER SEED

Sometimes mistakenly called thistle seed, niger seed is actually not the seed of a thistle, but of a plant (*Guizotia abyssinica*) grown in India and Ethiopia for use in cooking oil and soap. A small, black seed, it has long been used as a food for cage birds. In 1972, niger seed, along with a feeder for holding it, was

offered commercially for feeding wild birds, and has since become popular. Sixty percent of Project FeederWatch participants in the Northeast and South-Central regions offer niger seed at feeders. The American Goldfinch, Pine Siskin, Common Redpoll, Purple Finch, and House Finch are so eager for the seed that they will desert other foods to eat it. However, House Finches, when competing with goldfinches, tend to favor black-oil sunflower seed.

Another way to get around competition from House Finches is to offer niger seed in an "anti-House-Finch feeder." The perches of this feeder are above the feeding vents instead of below them. Users must hang by their feet in an inverted position to reach the openings! Goldfinches, as well as the Pine Siskin and Common Redpoll, often hang upside down to reach food in the wild. The House Finch is unable to perform this feat.

Niger seed that falls to the ground is readily consumed by the Mourning Dove, Dark-eyed Junco, native sparrows, and other finches. The small seeds are usually scorned by blackbirds and squirrels. Chickadees and titmice eat them but prefer sunflower seed.

Compared to other standard foods used in bird feeding, niger seed is expensive. However, a small amount of seed goes a long way. The seeds are eaten by only a select clientele and are so small that they cannot be consumed rapidly. It is wasteful to use niger seed in what are called thistle bags or stockings. Close to half the seed held in the woven mesh bags falls to the ground while birds are pecking at them.

Niger seed spoils readily when exposed to moisture. If it remains uneaten for several days, it has probably spoiled and the birds are refusing it. If this is the case, empty the feeder, clean it, and refill with fresh seed.

The arrival of a Red-headed Woodpecker is worth the small investment in sunflower seed, peanuts, corn, and other treats. A wire feeder is easy for woodpeckers to cling to while they extract food. The attached tray allows room for perching birds to clean up leftovers.

Black-oil sunflower seed is preferred by more birds than any other seed or grain. This finch mix is designed for goldfinches, House Finches, and Purple Finches. Millet is prized by juncos and sparrows. Inexpensive cracked corn is favored by undesirable birds as well as feeder favorites.

Black-oil sunflower   Finch mix   Millet   Cracked corn

SEEDS AND GRAINS
continued

CORN

Long a standard bird food, corn can be offered in many forms, from whole, dry cobs to cracked corn to cornmeal mush. Quail, doves, pigeons, the European Starling, the Northern Cardinal, blackbirds, and the House Sparrow favor cracked corn. Recipes using cornmeal and other corn products are popular with many birds that come to feeders. However, corn invites rodents and is subject to spoilage in damp weather. (Whole kernels keep better than cracked corn.) Corn is high in carbohydrates and raises body temperature, so use it primarily for winter bird feeding.

Whole, dried corncobs are an ideal and inexpensive squirrel food. Push the cobs onto spikes or hang them from a branch.

MIXED BIRDSEED

Nearly all ground-feeding birds find something in seed mixes, which usually include millet, milo, wheat, cracked corn, and canary seed, with a few black-oil sunflower seeds. Gourmet mixtures may contain such ingredients as almond meats and niger seed.

Inexpensive mixes often include many seeds that birds do not eat. Milo (a form of sorghum) is particularly prone to being wasted. However, in the Southwest, where it is widely grown, milo is popular with most ground-feeding birds.

In tests conducted by the U.S. Department of Agriculture, birds preferred black-oil sunflower to other sunflower seed and white proso to other millet. The same tests show that birds do not favor buckwheat, flax seed, milo, oats, wheat, rice, or rapeseed compared to other seeds and grain. However, don't give

The California Quail, a Pacific coast species, is a gregarious bird that travels in flocks called coveys. A swift runner but reluctant to fly, it prefers to feed on or near the ground.

up on other ingredients. Birds vary locally in their preference, and can surprise you.

Formulate your own bird-food mixture by using a testing tray, as explained on page 36, or try the recipes below. The chart on page 43 gives the food preferences of the most common seed-eating birds.

Offer mixed seed on the ground or on open trays or platforms near ground level. Research conducted by Project FeederWatch shows that mixed birdseed is the first choice of 21 species of birds that do most of their feeding on or near the ground. Offered at higher levels, mixed seed has far fewer takers.

NUTMEATS

Offer peanuts and tree nuts in winter, when birds most need the extra protein and calories in these highly nutritious foods. Nutmeats are subject to spoiling in hot, humid weather.

Birds like exotic nuts from other countries as well as native ones. Almonds, for example, native to Asia, are a favorite bird food.

If you give birds a little help, they will readily accept nutmeats in the shell. Break the shells of hickory nuts, black walnuts, almonds, and pecans with a hammer and let the birds pick out the meats.

Nutmeat or peanut feeders made of ¼-inch wire mesh are available at wild-bird centers. Hang the feeder from a horizontal line that has been squirrelproofed (see page 46) and watch chickadees, titmice, nuthatches, and wrens cling to the feeder and tug at the nutmeats inside. To prevent spoilage, bring the feeder inside when rain is imminent.

Birds are fond of peanuts, whether raw, roasted, or lightly salted. Those in the shell are usually carried away by jays, who bury them or pound them open. Peanut hearts—the embryos of the peanut, which are removed in making peanut butter—are the only peanut product that birds rarely eat.

RECOMMENDED BIRDSEED MIXES

Many excellent birdseed mixes are available commercially. If you make your own, you can best control the ingredients.

GENERAL MIX:
Sunflower seed (unhulled oil type) 50 percent
Millet (white proso) 35 percent
Cracked corn (fine or medium) 15 percent

FINCH AND CARDINAL MIX:
Black-oil sunflower seed 45 percent
Sunflower hearts 20 percent
Niger seed 20 percent
Safflower seed 15 percent

PURCHASING AND STORING BIRD FOOD

Three types of bird food most often available in stores are seeds, grains, and nutmeats. Suet and suet cakes can either be purchased or made at home. Where to buy these products, how much to buy, and how to store them are important considerations.

Purchase birdseed from a reputable supplier, such as specialty wild-bird stores, feed stores, nurseries, home and garden centers, or specialty mail-order companies. On page 92 you will find several mail-order sources listed. The ads of the magazines listed there often contain additional sources of birdseed available through the mail.

Buying food in bulk is more economical than in small amounts, but a large amount of seed requires ample storage space and involves the risk of damage from insects or dampness. Fortunately, many suppliers have sales at which you can buy large amounts at a time and store it at the supplier's location; you take delivery of small portions only as you need them. You save money and at the same time get fresh, safe food.

Inspect seed carefully for insect damage before bringing it home. Tiny, round holes in hulls are signs that the grain weevil is present and larvae have hatched. The larvae of this pest eat the kernel and leave only the empty hull. Another insect, the grain moth, leaves webby strands at the seams of the bag. Also check for a powder resembling sawdust, which may be the excrement of insect pests. If you find signs of infestation, return the seed and ask for a fresh replacement.

STORING FOOD

Store seed in a trash can with a tight lid in a cool, dry spot such as a garage or an unheated porch. Use metal trash cans, which deter rodents from gnawing through the container to reach the seed. Be sure the lid is tight-fitting, to prevent mice or raccoons from entering. Because grain moths could hatch and escape the seed bin, avoid storing seed near other foods.

Seeds and grains will last much longer in cool temperatures than warm temperatures and under dry conditions rather than damp conditions. Regardless of conditions, do not store food for longer than six months. *If food becomes moldy or shows signs of serious insect damage, throw it out.* Clean and disinfect the seed container before using it to store a fresh supply of seed.

Once the food has been placed in a feeder, it is subject to even greater hazards, particularly if birds do not eat it quickly. Food that is in open trays or on the ground is most subject to spoilage and contamination from droppings. Avoid ground-feeding if you live in a snowy area or experience wet winters, because wet seed quickly rots and molds.

To avoid problems offer small amounts of food at a time and clean these areas often. All feeders should be easy to clean.

Tubular feeders that hang from a branch or some other support offer the best protection from moisture and contamination. Hanging feeders with adjustable overhead domes also provide good protection from the elements and are reasonably squirrelproof.

Wooden hopper feeders, either hanging or on posts or platforms, are reasonably safe if all the food sifts out as birds eat their way through the supply. But if some of the food is left behind inside the hopper, it will decay and lead to a possible health hazard.

The bird foods that you need to be most careful with are niger seed, cracked corn, sunflower meats (and all "no-waste" mixes), black-oil sunflower seed, and nutmeats. Because these seeds and nutmeats lack a tight outer covering, they are susceptible to insect damage and spoilage.

Niger seed spoils quickly when exposed to moisture. Even the condensation inside a tube-type feeder will cause spoilage. If birds are no longer coming to feeders holding niger seed, the seed may have gone bad. Empty the feeder, clean it, and offer a fresh supply.

Problems of spoilage at the feeder or on the ground are all but eliminated if birds eat the food quickly. By keeping limited amounts of bird food on hand and offering only small amounts at a time, you can prevent spoilage and contamination problems.

RECOMMENDED STORAGE TIMES FOR BIRD FOODS

	One Month	Two Months	Three Months	Six Months
Niger seed	■			
Cracked corn	■			
Sunflower meats	■			
Nutmeats		■		
Black-oil sunflower seed			■	
Striped sunflower seed				■
Safflower seed				■
Millet, milo, or canary seed				■

SUET AND SUET MIXTURES

SUET AND PEANUT BUTTER RECIPES

Plain suet or beef fat from the butcher are appealing enough to make the suet feeder a popular spot. It is fun to make your own special suet-based treats, adding other foods that suet eaters enjoy. Hulled sunflower seed, chopped peanuts and nuts, and cracked corn are welcome, and birds can eat them whole. Peanut butter is a favorite addition; buy the chunky kind for extra tidbits. Cornmeal will help extend the mix and add nutrition. Chopped or whole small dried fruits are relished by many birds.

NO-MELT PEANUT BUTTER SUET

1 cup lard (no substitutes)
1 cup chunky peanut butter
2 cups quick-cooking oats
2 cups cornmeal
1 cup white flour
⅓ cup granulated sugar
In a large saucepan, melt lard and peanut butter, then stir in the remaining ingredients. Pour this mixture into square freezer containers to form a suet layer about 1½ inches thick. Store in the freezer. Cut into cakes and place into wire feeder. The suet cakes will not melt in typical summer or warm winter weather.

SOFT PEANUT BUTTER MIX

1 cup freshly ground suet
1 cup peanut butter
3 cups yellow cornmeal
½ cup enriched white or whole wheat flour
In a large saucepan, melt suet, then add peanut butter, stirring until melted and well blended. Let the suet mixture cool and start to thicken, then add the corn meal and flour and blend. Let cool. Pack into feeders or smear on pinecones or tree trunks.

The aptly named Yellow-bellied Sapsucker eats suet and seeds at feeders and drills for sap.

WINTER SUET MIX

4 cups melted suet
2 cups chunky peanut butter
¾ cup dark brown sugar
1½ cup cornmeal
Water as needed
1 cup sunflower hearts
1 cup chopped dried fruit

Stir suet, peanut butter, and brown sugar in top of a double boiler until blended. Add cornmeal and enough water to allow you to stir in sunflower hearts and dried fruit. Pour into molds or directly into feeders.

Among people who feed birds, the popularity of suet, along with that of mixed birdseed, is second only to that of black-oil sunflower seed. Suet is used more often in the North than the South.

Woodpeckers, chickadees, nuthatches, titmice, and starlings are fond of suet. Bluebirds and Carolina Wrens may also eat their share, especially in winter when insects are scarce. Juncos and other birds that can't cling to a suet feeder may gather bits that fall below the feeder.

Beef suet is the best type for birds, and you can purchase it at low cost from a butcher. Be sure to ask for short suet, or kidney suet, rather than stringy suet. Make sure that it is fresh, firm, and white. If you intend to melt it down, ask the butcher to grind it for you, or grind it yourself with a kitchen grinder.

PREPARING SUET

To make suet cakes, you must first melt the fat. Fill the lower container of a double boiler with water. Place the ground suet in the top container and let the water boil. Heat the suet until it has been rendered to a liquid. Allow hot suet to cool and thicken before adding other ingredients. Raisins, peanut butter, refined corn products, and a variety of fruits are among the bird treats you can stir into the thickening suet before pouring it into forms or packing it into bird feeders. (See the suet recipes at left.) Placing seeds in suet mixtures is inadvisable. Mixed birdseed is for ground-feeding birds and only gets in the way when added to suet cakes.

Ground suet can be purified by heating it, as described previously, allowing it to cool and solidify, then removing the fat that has risen to the surface and letting it drain. You can store purified suet in the refrigerator or reheat it immediately and make it into cakes.

Compared to unpurified suet, purified suet makes harder cakes that last much longer outdoors. Using purified suet is essential when offering suet in spring and summer. In hot weather offer suet in the shade only. If melting occurs bring the holder and suet cake indoors and refrigerate them. Follow the same procedure at night in any season if nocturnal mammals are a problem. If starlings are a problem, use any one of several starling-proof suet feeders now on the market.

Commercial suet cakes are widely available, and most have the advantage of being highly refined and relatively hard, characteristics that retard spoilage. They also tend to fit neatly into commercial suet feeders. Many birds prefer the softer homemade mixtures, however, and the treats you add to them.

OTHER FOODS

FRUIT AND JELLY

Fruit and jelly attract birds that may not otherwise visit the feeder—especially in summer, when fruit-eating birds from the Tropics appear, and in winter, when mockingbirds, orioles, catbirds, or robins are in the vicinity. There is nothing like a halved orange impaled on a twig or nail (or at a feeder designed to hold oranges) to lure an oriole. A shallow bowl of cut-up fruit with globs of jelly on the side may also bring interesting visitors. Replenish the supply frequently in freezing weather.

Raisins and dried currants attract, among others, Cedar and Bohemian Waxwings—about the hardest birds to attract. Steam or soak the raisins or currants to soften, and offer them in shallow containers. Once waxwings discover the food, they keep coming back for more. Sliced apple is another favored food.

As the chart on page 43 shows, fruit also attracts the Hermit Thrush, Scarlet Tanager, Cactus Wren, Yellow-rumped Warbler, Gray Catbird, Indigo Bunting, bluebirds, and many woodpeckers.

SUGAR WATER

Specialized hummingbird feeders are exploitable by many other birds, although sugar water is little more than a quick source of energy and not a substitute for other foods. Among nonhummingbird guests, orioles are the most common (manufacturers even offer special oriole feeders with properly spaced perches). Other visitors include the Rose-breasted Grosbeak, Northern Cardinal, Purple Finch, House Finch, American Goldfinch, and woodpeckers, titmice, chickadees, jays, warblers, and tanagers. Altogether, 53 bird species, other than hummingbirds, have been observed at sugar-water feeders.

MEALWORMS

Highly desirable to some hard-to-attract birds, mealworms are the segmented whitish larvae of darkling beetles, common pests of commercial grain storage areas. Bluebirds are drawn to a shallow dish regularly stocked with mealworms. Purple Martins, orioles, warblers, tanagers, and many other birds may also visit mealworm offerings, especially during nesting season. Buy mealworms from mail-order houses, some wild-bird supply stores, or fishing bait shops. Keep extra larvae in a plastic bucket filled with a few inches of cornmeal and topped by a tight-fitting lid. As the larvae mature, emerging adult beetles will mate and begin the cycle over again, renewing your supply of bird food.

BAKED GOODS

Birds have a special fondness for baked goods. Birds particularly favor white-bread crumbs, but they also eat pie crust, pancakes, corn bread, doughnuts, and cake and cracker crumbs. Doughnuts keep longer than other baked goods, and they may attract such unusual visitors as bluebirds, kinglets, warblers, and orioles. Offer baked goods in an open tray feeder or wire mesh feeder, or thread a doughnut onto the hook at the end of a straightened wire coat hanger. Discard uneaten baked goods before mold sets in.

Unfortunately, baked goods may invite unwanted guests to the bird feeder. House Sparrows, starlings, dogs, and cats are quick to spot baked goods in unprotected feeders.

Doughnuts are high-fat, high-carbohydrate snacks for this Western Scrub-Jay. Chickadees, bluebirds, and other favorite birds also like baked goods, but so do starlings, House Sparrows, and other undesirables.

An apple a day is key to attracting mockingbirds such as the one shown here. Fruit lures catbirds, robins, orioles, and many birds that rarely visit seed feeders, including the beautiful Varied Thrush of the Northwest.

Even without a convenient perch, nectar feeders made for hummingbirds are known to be used by at least 53 other species of birds in North America. This Orange-crowned Warbler is adept at sipping on the wing.

The best bait for bluebirds, such as the Western Bluebird shown here, is a dish of mealworms, the larvae of a common beetle. Place a feeder near bluebird habitat, and they may soon become regulars.

FOOD PRESENTATION

Many kinds of platform feeders are available commercially (see sources, page 92). Note the wire anti-squirrel guard on the tray at right; a smaller grid on the hanging feeder, left, also keeps out larger birds. What looks like a birdhouse is actually a feeder for bluebirds; they enter through the side holes to dine on mealworms and raisins inside.

How food is presented is nearly as important as the type of food offered. Fortunately, the human goal of having birds where we can see them usually coincides with avian preferences; most birds like having their food in the open. Some, such as doves and native sparrows, prefer to feed on or near the ground; others, such as titmice and chickadees, prefer higher feeders. For this reason, present food at different elevations.

To prevent crowding at the feeder, provide as many feeders as the size of the outdoor space and your inclinations allow. Some should be in windows or close to them. Place others well away from windows (for information on avoiding window strikes, see page 46). Place plantings near feeders so birds will have shelter from attack by predators.

CHOOSING FEEDERS

Feeders should be attractive, long-lasting, weatherproof, and open enough for you to see the birds eating at them. Birds are much more visible at some feeders, such as open tray or platform types, than at others. In protecting feeders against the weather and inroads by squirrels and other undesirable visitors, designers have been forced to make feeders that are less open. Some models are so closed that humans have trouble seeing the birds and the birds have trouble reaching the food.

Of course, presenting food to birds does not have to involve a bird feeder. You can offer food on a roof, balcony, patio, or deck, or on a natural object such as a rock or a hollow in a log. Suet mixtures can be smeared into crevices in the bark of tree trunks.

If you are setting up your first feeder, start with one in which food is readily visible to birds flying nearby. An open tray or a platform feeder is ideal for the initial offering. Finches seem to quickly recognize tube feeders. Generally, birds will find a new feeder within a week or less.

Some commercial bird feeders are shown below and on pages 44 and 45. Building your own feeders is a quick project if you have carpentry tools and skills. For a variety of plans and instructions, consult the Ortho book *Building Birdhouses and Feeders*.

PLATFORM FEEDERS

BIRD-FEEDER PLACEMENT

Select a spot for your feeding station that allows you a clear view of the activity from a comfortable viewing spot. A feeder outside your kitchen window, where you can watch birds while you enjoy your morning coffee, might be ideal. If you spend a lot of time in the garden, you may want to place feeders where they can be seen easily from a bench or patio area. Be sure your selected spot offers nearby cover for protection from predators, and shrubs or trees that shelter it from wind.

Most birds will travel at least a short distance to reach a feeding area, but if you are trying to lure shy birds from wild places nearby, it is a good idea to place feeders near their natural habitat, at least at first. Once birds are accustomed to visiting the feeder, gradually move it closer to the house. Remember, though, that birds are creatures of habit and don't respond well to abrupt changes in the position of feeders.

VARIETY AND ABUNDANCE

Attract the most birds by offering a variety of feeding spots and types of feeders. Be sure your feeders are sheltered from wind, especially in winter. Besides making birds uncomfortable, strong winds can disturb hanging feeders and scatter the food. A well-rounded bird-feeding program includes several feeding stations: a platform feeder on a post about 5 feet off the ground, a few hopper or tube feeders 5 to 8 feet above the ground (with a tube feeder used for niger seed), a window feeder, and suet feeders mounted on tree trunks at various heights. Make use of natural "platforms" you already have to support platform feeders. These include tree stumps, flat rocks, walls, and fence posts.

If you have the space, establish two or three feeding areas about 50 feet apart, each with a variety of feeders at different heights. This allows you to cater to the preferences of different bird species by taking advantage of the different types of plantings in your landscape, such as meadow gardens, shrub borders, or woodland. Offering several feeding areas also solves many problems of unruly behavior; the aggressive individual that chases off other birds will be unable to defend several feeding areas at once.

Consider the task of refilling when you place your feeders. Make sure you can reach your feeders on a blustery, cold day or in deep snow or ice, the times when birds most heavily use feeders. Keep at least one large feeder within easy reach of the house for times when bad weather makes refilling difficult.

FAVORITE FOODS OF FEEDER BIRDS AND LEVELS AT WHICH THEY FEED

Knowledge about food preferences is far from complete. Many birds will try foods other than those known to be their favorites. Most birds accept food at different levels but generally display a preference for eating either at ground or near-ground level, or at an elevated site.

Bird	Safflower	Sunflower	Niger	Corn	Mixed Seed*	Nutmeats	Suet & Mixes	Bakery Goods	Fruit	Sugar Water	Raised Feeders	Ground Feeders
Bluebirds						■	■		■		■	
Bunting, Indigo		■			■	■			■			■
Bunting, Lazuli					■							■
Cardinal, Northern	■	■			■	■	■		■		■	■
Catbird, Gray							■	■	■	■	■	
Chickadees		■				■	■				■	
Creeper, Brown						■	■					
Dove, Mourning		■	■	■	■							■
Finch, House		■	■		■						■	■
Finch, Purple	■	■	■		■						■	■
Flicker, Northern				■			■	■	■			■
Goldfinch, American		■	■		■						■	■
Grosbeak, Evening		■									■	■
Grosbeak, Rose-breasted	■	■				■					■	
Jay, Blue		■		■	■	■	■	■			■	■
Jay, Steller's		■		■		■					■	■
Junco, Dark-eyed		■	■		■							■
Kinglet, Ruby-crowned							■		■	■		
Mockingbird, Northern							■	■	■	■	■	
Nuthatch, Red-breasted		■				■	■				■	
Nuthatch, White-breasted		■				■	■				■	
Orioles					■				■	■	■	
Pigeon, Band-tailed				■	■							■
Quail, California					■	■						■
Redpoll, Common		■	■		■						■	■
Robin, American									■	■	■	
Sapsucker, Yellow-bellied							■	■	■	■		
Scrub-Jay, Western		■		■		■						■
Siskin, Pine		■	■	■	■	■					■	■
Sparrows (American)		■	■		■						■	■
Tanager, Scarlet							■		■	■	■	
Thrashers						■	■	■	■		■	
Thrush, Hermit							■	■	■			■
Titmice		■				■	■			■	■	
Towhees		■			■	■			■			■
Warbler, Orange-crowned							■			■	■	
Warbler, Yellow-rumped					■		■		■	■	■	■
Woodpecker, Downy				■		■	■		■		■	
Woodpecker, Hairy		■					■		■		■	
Woodpecker, Red-bellied		■		■		■	■	■	■		■	
Woodpecker, Red-headed		■		■		■	■		■		■	
Wren, Cactus							■	■	■		■	■
Wren, Carolina		■				■	■	■	■	■	■	
Wrentit							■					

*Mixed seed is defined here as being composed of 90% millet. Other ingredients—such as milo, wheat, cracked corn, and canary seed—comprise the remaining 10%.

HOPPER AND TUBE FEEDERS

Hinge for top

7"   9"

Hook and eye

6¾"

4¾"

6¼"

7½"   8"

6¾"

7"

1½"   3"   1½"

6¾"   5½"

7"   6"

Hopper and tube feeders dole out seed as birds consume it, thus reducing waste and deterring feeder-hogging squirrels. Squirrel baffles (1, 4, 6, and 10) and squirrel cones (3, 10) provide even more anti-pest protection; counterweighted feeders (5) and wire guard "Havens" (2) are the most effective of all. A niger-seed sack (7) attracts goldfinches but can waste seed. Wobbly hanging globes (8) are for chickadees. A rough wood feeder with room for a tail prop (6) is tailor-made for woodpeckers. Choose well-constructed commercial hopper feeders (9), or build your own from the plan at right, using acrylic plastic for the sliding hopper door. For sources of the bird feeders shown on pages 44 and 45, please see page 92.

CONSTRUCTION PLAN FOR BASIC HOPPER FEEDER

SUET, FRUIT, AND NECTAR FEEDERS

CONSTRUCTION PLAN FOR BASIC SUET FEEDER

Hinge for top

3½" 5"

Hook and eye

5"
3½"
7"
11"
8"
1"
5"
5" 1½"

Commercial suet feeders come in all shapes and sizes, but most follow the principle of holding a block of solid fat securely while birds peck at it. You can build your own feeder with basic tools and beginner skills, using the plan shown at left. Some suet feeders (3, 5) come with effective wire guards that discourage squirrels and large birds from raiding the larder. Some are designed for woodpeckers, either by offering the suet from the bottom of the feeder (4) or providing a surface area for a tail to prop against (10, 7). And some feeders are made for smearing on soft suet or peanut butter (11). Fruit feeders (2, 6) offer a sturdy spike for impaling fruit, plus a perch for access. Some (6) provide pockets for globs of jelly. Nectar feeders may accommodate one to several guests. Although most are intended for hummingbirds (9, 12), some are made for orioles (6). And finally, in this smorgasbord of feeders, we have included two for those amusing customers, squirrels (1, 8).

KEEPING THE PEACE

If you are feeding birds for the first time, you may be surprised to discover that playing host to birds calls for mediation skills. You may have to keep the peace among birds as well as negotiate with your neighbors.

Let birds in and keep squirrels out with sturdy wire guards.

BIRD ARBITRATION

Squirrels, chipmunks, and some birds take more than their share if you let them. Preventing a few species from interfering with your feeding program can be difficult, and it takes patience. Vary the foods, feeders, and feeder placement until you achieve the desired balance. Target the species you want to attract by offering its favorite foods. In the "Gallery of Birds" starting on page 66 you will find the specific food preferences of 75 birds that people most want to attract.

RELATIONSHIPS WITH NEIGHBORS

Prevent fatal window strikes with netting.

Bird-feeding activities might cause problems with your neighbors because of the birds that flock to the area, splattering cars or laundry with droppings or the debris from bird feeders. Tall barriers, such as a hedge or fence, might help keep ground feeders out of the neighbor's yard. If debris is a problem, switch to seeds that have had their hulls removed, such as sunflower meats or no-waste mixes. This is also a good solution if you feed birds from a balcony or high-rise window.

WINDOW STRIKES

Collisions with windows can cause death or injury to birds. Birds see the reflection of the landscape instead of seeing the glass, and they fly toward it. Minimize collisions by placing feeders in or next to windows or else 25 feet or more away. If birds take off close to a window when startled, they can't gain enough momentum to harm themselves. If you find a bird that is only stunned, place it in a paper bag, twist the top, and give it time to recover. When you hear it moving, take it to a door or window and release it.

Lure squirrels, jays, and crows away with corn.

To prevent window strikes, screen the window with netting. Hang bird netting (the kind used to protect fruit trees from birds) from the eaves or just outside the window. Weight the bottom or staple it to keep it taut, and it will be almost invisible. Silhouettes of hawks or owls placed on the glass, and ribbons, tinsel, or strips of tape on the window, are often ineffective; netting is the best solution.

SQUIRREL-PROOFING

Squirrels are delightful animals that are as enjoyable to watch as birds. Unfortunately, squirrels are voracious eaters and can empty a feeder in a short time. Because squirrels like most of the same foods as birds, they can become pests at bird feeders. Divert them by offering them their own feeder, and keep them from raiding bird feeders by using a variety of anti-squirrel devices.

A squirrel-feeding station placed at some distance from bird feeders will help keep squirrels from raiding the birds' food. Corn is an inexpensive squirrel food. Skewer an ear of dried corn on a nail driven through the middle of a platform from the bottom, or insert a screw eye into one end of a cob and hang the cob from a hook where squirrels can reach it. Many different squirrel feeders are available. Some force squirrels to perform amusing antics for their food.

Squirrels are agile and persistent acrobats. They can jump upward as much as 4 feet and horizontally as much as 8 feet. They can balance on a wire and can climb anything that gives them the slightest grip. To protect a bird feeder mounted on a pole, place the pole at least 8 feet from anything the squirrel could use as a launching platform for a long leap to the feeder. Keep squirrels from climbing the pole by installing a metal or plastic barricade at least 4 feet above the ground. Make the barricade by wrapping sheet metal around the pole, in a cone shape, with the open end of the cone facing down. Or purchase a plastic or metal barricade made for this purpose.

Hanging feeders can be squirrelproofed with a commercially available plastic guard hung from the wire above the feeder.

If your feeder is hung from a horizontal wire between two points, keep squirrels from walking on the wire by covering it with plastic tubing, such as that used in irrigation systems, for several feet on each side of the feeder. The slippery, smooth tubing will spin under the squirrel's feet, dumping the animal off the wire.

Many squirrel-proof bird feeders are available (see pages 42, 44, and 45). Most keep out squirrels, but some are unattractive and some restrict your view of the birds feeding. If you wish to place a feeder in a tree or another place that gives squirrels easy access, however, a squirrel-proof feeder is the only way to keep squirrels from raiding the birds' food.

PREDATION

Bird-watchers often feel responsible if a hawk or a cat kills a bird in their yard or garden. However, studies have shown that the number of birds killed in the vicinity of feeders is actually lower than the number killed in the wild. This may be because birds at feeders obtain their food in a relatively short time and can devote more time to watching for predators. And it may be because most feeders are placed in the open where cats are not as successful at hunting.

Predation is a natural part of birds' lives. A high reproductive rate helps make up for losses from predation, accidents, disease, and weather. Normally, the heaviest losses occur at the nest during the fledgling stage. The young birds' inexperience and poor flying make them easy prey. Birds that survive this period have a fair chance of living much longer. Many of the same birds that spend the winter or summer in your yard come back year after year.

Predation keeps birds alert and helps keep the species strong and fit. Nevertheless, seeing a bird you have come to love be eaten by a hawk or killed by a cat is distressing. Most people who feed birds want to help protect their guests from predators.

CATS

Although not all cats kill birds, many of them do. Take these steps with your own cat and suggest them to your neighbors, too.
■ Keep cats indoors as much as possible—especially at night and during nesting season. Your cat will live longer, too, if it stays inside.
■ Use hanging bird feeders and place them no closer to the ground than 4 feet.
■ Place birdbaths and feeders near trees but well away (at least 6 feet) from dense shrubs.
■ Call on the services of a yappy dog to keep cats out of your yard.
■ Work in your community for the passage of cat neutering and licensing laws.

HAWKS

Hawks are seen near feeders more frequently today than in the past. If a hawk begins visiting regularly, the best course is to stop feeding the birds for a few days. They will disperse in search of natural foods, and the hawk will leave to hunt elsewhere, after which you can resume feeding. Dense cover near feeders helps birds escape hawk attacks but encourages cat attacks. Placing feeders about 6 to 12 feet from shrubby cover helps birds escape both hawks and cats.

Help prevent greasy feathers by using firm, hard suet.

Cute but lethal: Keep Kitty out of the feeder and in the house.

SAFE AND SANITARY

The appearance of a sick, slow-moving bird that stays behind when others fly away serves as a warning: Conditions at the feeder could be the cause of the illness. Where birds congregate and bird droppings accumulate, unsanitary conditions can foster the spread of disease. By taking precautions, you can prevent the outbreak of several bird diseases.

UNSAFE FOODS

For the most part, birds instinctively know what is good for them and avoid foods that are harmful. Take the responsibility for ensuring that food offered in your feeders is safe.

Messy foods, such as kitchen leftovers or overripe fruit, can lead to unsanitary conditions and attract nuisance species. It is best not to offer these foods.

Suet that begins to liquefy in hot summer weather can mat the breast and chin feathers of some birds, such as woodpeckers. Use the appropriate suet mixture for summer and present it properly.

Do not offer peanuts or coconut in summer. Peanuts become rancid in hot, wet weather.

Also, British researchers have found that nestling titmice are unable to digest fat, and oil-rich peanuts and coconut were harmful to young in their early stages of development.

Use corn sparingly in summer. It elevates body temperature and spoils easily.

Wild black cherries, pyracantha berries, and other fruits may ferment on the plant, causing the birds that eat them to become intoxicated. American Robins and Cedar Waxwings are the most often affected. They become woozy, often flying into houses or oncoming traffic. Residents of California have come to expect these binges at about the same time every winter; comparable sights are seen wherever pyracantha is commonly grown.

Many other fruits ferment and cause similar problems, including apple, pear, blueberry and mountain ash (*Sorbus* spp.), as well as some exotic, invasive (but unfortunately common) plants such as Brazilian pepper tree (*Schinus terebinthifolius*) and Chinaberry (*Melia azedarach*). Drape these bushes and trees with bird netting, if possible, as soon as intoxication is noted.

Feeder birds are a full-course dinner to Sharp-shinned Hawks.

PROVIDING WATER

This female Northern Cardinal has found the perfect bathing spot. Only when a bird feels secure in its surroundings, and only after it has checked for predators, will it abandon itself to a bath with wholehearted vigor. Even then, it may frequently pause to scan for danger.

THE JOYS OF WATER

Water—in a fountain, pool, or birdbath—is as irresistible to birds as it is to people. In the arid parts of the West, water is a scarce resource for birds; it is the most important thing you can offer to attract them. Even in the moist Northeast and Northwest, water in the form birds prefer can be hard to find. Especially during long dry spells and in winter when water is frozen, birds may have a long search for a chance to drink and bathe.

By including a reliable source of fresh water in your garden year-round, you will provide for the needs of your regular visitors and increase the possibility of attracting birds you don't usually see. Warblers, swallows, and other birds that eat insects almost exclusively and are difficult to attract with feeders may be drawn to your garden by water.

There are many ways to provide water for birds while enhancing the beauty of the home landscape. Artificial "rain puddles," or birdbaths, are available in a huge variety of sizes, forms, and materials. If you have a garden pool, adapt it to the special needs of birds. If you're starting from scratch, you can easily construct a simple pool. A water-filled plastic tub, old wine barrel or bathtub, scooped-out log, simple hole in the ground lined with plastic, or garden hose with a mist sprayer can entice birds to your home.

FRESH WATER ALL YEAR LONG

However you present it, water should be fresh, clean, and abundant. Hose off and refill birdbaths often. In hot weather check them daily to make sure they are full. Periodically clean and refill garden pools. A circulating pump and the addition of plants will help keep water fresh and clear. Water intended for birds is no place for chemicals of any kind. Never add chemicals to it to control algae or insects or prevent freezing.

Water should be available and accessible in all seasons. One of the prime attractions of water you provide is its reliability; natural sources tend to shift, dry up, or freeze with changing weather. The birdbath is popular even in the coldest days of winter, and it's important to keep it unfrozen. Birdbaths and small pools can be thawed by pouring a kettle of boiling water in them, but this is tedious to do on a regular basis.

A simple way to provide fresh water in cold weather is to use a passive solar-heated birdbath. Any birdbath constructed of thick stone or concrete with a dark basin will work.

The dark color and mass helps it absorb heat from the sun, then slowly release it as a kind of low-tech natural heater. Placed in an area that gets full sun, this kind of birdbath is effective when the temperature hovers just below freezing. Where winters are colder, you will need to invest in an electric-powered heater for your birdbath.

The most convenient way to keep birdbath water from freezing is to use an immersion water heater designed specifically for outdoor use. Several varieties are available in garden-supply stores and hardware centers. Some are designed for water deeper than that usually found in birdbaths and are more appropriate for pools and tubs. For the shallow water of a birdbath or garden pool, purchase a version to operate at a depth of 1½ to 3 inches. It should have an automatic thermostat that shuts off the heating element when the water reaches 40 degrees F. If an extension cord is needed, be sure to use the heavy-duty exterior kind with a triple-pronged, grounded plug. Heating tapes are also available for use in birdbaths, but they are appropriate only in mild climates with occasional freezes.

An alternative to placing a water heater in the birdbath is to buy a bath with a heating unit already installed and completely hidden. You can plug the bath into an electrical outlet whenever temperatures drop below freezing. Both pedestal and dish baths having this feature are available at wild-bird centers and garden stores.

The cheerful, active American Goldfinch will regularly visit your garden for water.

A simple, inexpensive immersion heater keeps water from freezing in winter, providing liquid refreshment for this female Northern Cardinal and other birds.

ACCESSIBILITY

When water is scarce in the wild, birds seek the vital liquid wherever they can find it. A forgotten bucket, a trickle of water from an air-conditioner outlet, or a pet's outside water dish may become an impromptu watering hole for garden birds. When you are devising a long-term water source for your garden, plan for the type of water feature that birds adopt most quickly: a shallow, rough-bottomed pool of still water.

The surface of the container, where birds enter the water, should be rough, to provide sure footing. Textured materials appropriate for birdbaths, pools, and streams include sand, stone, pebbles, and concrete. Make smooth, slippery surfaces such as plastic or metal more attractive to birds by using coarse sandpaper to roughen them or attaching the kind of textured footing used in bathtubs. Some of the prettiest birdbaths are made of smooth, glazed clay, a surface that does not offer sure footing. Scatter a few handfuls of coarse gravel into such birdbaths to help birds get a better grip, or settle a rock in the center so that birds can at least come to drink.

The water container should have a gradual, shallow slope. Almost all garden birds prefer water that is no deeper than 2 to 3 inches, and some like it even shallower. Don't buy a birdbath any deeper than 3 inches, and select one that approaches this depth gradually. The depth should increase only 1 inch in 8 inches. A lip or other perch where birds can alight before entering the water is an advantage, as is a dry, flat space on which they can hop to the edge of the water. If birds are reluctant to use your birdbath, try adding a few rocks or a brick for secure footing.

Garden pools created from preformed liners are popular with gardeners but less so with birds, because the depth drops suddenly near the edge of the water. You can adapt such a pool for bird-bathing and -drinking by placing good-size rocks or bricks at one end beneath the water, until you have built a stable area on top of which the water is only a couple of inches deep. It is a good idea to allow the rocks that define the limit of the shallow area to protrude several inches above the water, so that they act as a barrier to bathing birds, keeping them in the shallow end of the pool.

Large ponds often have a naturally shallow area around the edges, which birds eagerly make use of. If your pond is ringed by tall grass or other vegetation, consider laying a beach of native pebbles in one section so that birds have a clear view of predators, and you have a clear view of bathing birds.

A family of California Quail seeks water in this appealing California garden. Plenty of open space is interspersed with cover such as the clump of agapanthus near a ground pool, backed with fiery red hummingbird sage (Dicliptera suberecta).

SAFETY AND VISIBILITY

Safety is a prime consideration in placing a water source. A wet bird, preoccupied with bathing and slowed by wet feathers, is a vulnerable target for cats or hawks. Birds are well aware of potential predator danger and will hesitate to use a bathing spot that does not feel safe.

Most birds prefer a high perch and dense cover about 15 feet away from the water so that they can examine the area for possible danger and return to a refuge for preening. A few birds, however (especially birds of the forest floor, such as thrushes), prefer secret forest pools and quiet streams that are close to cover. These shy birds are more likely to visit a birdbath or garden pool hidden in dense shrubbery. If cats are not a threat in your garden, include a ground-level pool among sheltering vegetation, and you may enjoy unusual guests such as towhees and the Scarlet Tanager, forest dwellers that are reluctant to drink or bathe in the open.

If cats roam your neighborhood, keep your birdbath in the open, with no close shrubs behind which a predatory cat can lurk or overhanging limbs from which it can pounce. In areas where hawks are more of a menace than cats, close cover is a necessity for allowing birds a quick escape from danger.

Height gives added protection to birds. If your birdbath is near dense vegetation, and cats are a problem, raise the birdbath off the ground about 3 feet. In the open, ground-level birdbaths and pools are acceptable. A cat that is exposed rarely gets close enough to be a threat to birds.

Watching birds drink and splash is gratifying, so be sure to place the birds' water source where it is visible and convenient for you. Establish it near a place you use a lot, such as the house, patio, or sitting area. Keep in mind views from indoors too. Avoid masking your line of sight with dense vegetation.

Water for birds should be as close to a faucet as possible, so you don't have to lug a heavy hose for cleaning and refilling. A shady spot will minimize the growth of algae, but you will still want to clean the birdbath frequently so that birds are assured of fresh water. In summer, empty and refill the bath every three days to prevent mosquitoes from using the water as a breeding pool.

Consider your own safety, too, when choosing a site for a birdbath. Place ground-level or low baths away from garden paths, to avoid stumbling over them or damaging them with a wheelbarrow or lawn mower. Keep pedestal-type birdbaths, which are easily tipped, away from children's play areas.

A classic pedestal-type birdbath in another area of the California garden shown on page 50 is visited by a White-crowned Sparrow. Other sparrows, California Quail, and a Red-winged Blackbird forage on the open ground nearby.

BIRDBATHS

How you decide to provide water for birds will depend on the time and money you wish to spend rigging the water supply, the time you are willing to devote to maintenance, and what you find appropriate and beautiful for your yard.

A birdbath is the easiest way to set up a water source for birds. Birdbaths are available in a variety of ornamental styles that range from simple, natural containers of stone or wood to colorful, elaborate sculptures. Don't buy a birdbath with moving, shiny parts that might frighten birds. Otherwise, give your aesthetic sense free rein.

One aspect of birdbath design is how the basin is supported. Some birdbaths are simple dishes to set on the ground or on a windowsill or deck. Some hang by chains from a balcony, an eave, or a wall bracket. Others attach to a window with suction cups. The most common type is set on a pedestal, which raises it about 3 feet off the ground. Heavy stone, ceramic, or concrete dishes should have a broad, sturdy support. Metal, plastic, or wooden birdbaths should be firmly anchored to the pedestal or be of single-piece construction.

As long as its edge slopes gradually, the basin size is not crucial. However, a basin less than 12 inches across is generally too small, and baths or pools less than 18 inches in diameter will usually be used by only one bird at a time. Most birdbaths are 24 to 36 inches in diameter. This seems to be a good size for community bathing.

BIRDBATH MATERIALS

Birdbaths are available in a range of materials. Terra-cotta and glazed ceramic birdbaths are attractive but crack easily when the water in them freezes. Concrete and cement birdbaths are the most common types available, and their rough texture is a decided advantage.

The solid, heavy construction of concrete withstands freezing better than terra-cotta, glazed ceramic, or cement (cement is concrete without reinforcing gravel), although it may also crack under repeated freezes. Beautiful but costly granite birdbaths are the most durable.

Plastic and metal birdbaths withstand all kinds of weather, but their surfaces are too slippery unless they are textured. Their light weight makes them easy to handle but requires a firm support to keep them from tipping. Metal birdbaths should be made of

Choose a birdbath that suits your style, as well as the needs of your birds. Hanging baths are perfect for small decks. Larger baths act as focal points in the garden. Ground pools can be tucked away in a secluded spot. Investigate accessories, too, such as a dripper tube, which adds the allure of running water; a mister, for a soft, fine spray; and an immersion heater. For sources of these and other birdbaths, see page 92.

stainless steel or coated with rust-resistant paint. Painted metal birdbaths will eventually chip and flake and need repainting.

A few birdbaths sold commercially are made entirely of wood. They are difficult to keep clean, and even those made from rot-resistant wood, such as redwood or cedar, won't last as long as other kinds of birdbaths. They are generally well liked by birds, however, and can be attractive.

MAKING YOUR OWN BIRDBATH

With a little imagination you can easily make your own birdbath. Any kind of dish with a gradual slope, a lip for perching, and the appropriate depth and dimensions can be used. The kind of saucer placed under potted plants can make an excellent tiny birdbath. A 3-foot log, cut square on both ends, makes a good pedestal. A log of close-grained wood, such as oak or hickory, can be hollowed out with a chisel to contain water. A large stone that has a natural depression to hold water can be an attractive addition to your garden.

When birds bathe, particularly in large numbers at a time, they can get quite excited and energetic, splashing water all about. Unless you want a soggy, muddy area around the bath, set it on a pad that will quickly absorb or drain off water. Gravel or sand drain well. For a 30-inch birdbath, remove about 4 inches of soil from an area about 4 feet square. Refill the depression with dark-colored river gravel, pea gravel, or sand. Set the birdbath in place so that it is level.

A nearby shrub provides a perch for after-bath preening. If skulking cats are a possibility, keep the bath 6 to 12 feet away from the shrub so that predators can't ambush vulnerable birds in the bath.

Misters break a stream of water into fine droplets, offering a gentle shower that hummingbirds, robins, and other garden birds find delightful. Direct the spray into an open area, where birds have room to fly through the mist or splash about beneath it, or aim the mist over a birdbath.

SMALL POOLS

Bushtits congregate in a small pool to splash and drink. This tiny, sociable relative of chickadees travels in flocks through thickets of the western coast, deserts, and mountains.

A small pool useful to birds can be nothing more than a birdbath set into the ground. Some pools are large enough for fish and water plants.

The easiest kind of small pool to provide is the basin of a birdbath; heavy concrete ones work best. Dig a depression deep enough so that the lip of the basin extends about 2 inches above ground level. The lip will prevent soil from washing in. Set the basin in place and backfill around the edges, and you have a small garden pool in a matter of minutes. Use a strong spray from a hose to rinse old water out of this pool without lifting it from the ground. Include moisture-loving plants nearby, such as cardinal flower (*Lobelia cardinalis*) or rushes (*Juncus* spp.), which will thrive on the extra water from frequent cleaning.

BUILDING A POOL

To build a small garden pool whose basin is the earth itself, begin by digging out the soil to any depth and shape you wish. Use some of the earth you dig up to build a small mound about 6 inches higher than ground level and about 12 inches wide all the way around the edge. Tamp the soil in the depression and compress the mounded edge. While you are tamping, create a small trench around the outside edge of the mound. The trench should be about 4 inches deep and extend 6 inches out from the mound. Line the depression with an old carpet liner, followed by a black flexible pond liner (available at many garden and home centers). The carpet liner will prevent rocks from damaging the flexible liner. Allow the edge of the flexible liner to extend into the trench, and cover it with gravel. Now you are ready to fill your pool

These Northern Mockingbirds have found the perfect place for a satisfying sip of water or a quick bath. Shallow water, gently sloping sides, and solid, textured footing encourage birds to visit pools in the wild and in gardens. A log provides a natural perch for birds to preen or keep a lookout.

with water. Line the sides and top of the edges with flat rocks to help hold the liner in place and disguise the edges. Set the rocks in place carefully so they don't tear the liner.

A bit more expensive, but also more permanent, is a preformed liner made of fiberglass or rigid plastic, available at garden centers and hardware stores. Be sure to purchase one in which at least a part of the pool is shallow enough to be appropriate for birds. Simply dig out soil to accommodate the shape of the pool, set the pool in place, and fill it with water. Place rocks along the rim to hide the edges of the pool and make it look more interesting. If necessary, set flat rocks in the pool to provide birds a gradual approach to the water.

LANDSCAPING THE POOL

Make a garden pool look like a delightfully natural element of the garden by choosing a varied edging. Instead of surrounding the pool with a ring of rocks all about the same size, stagger smaller rocks with larger boulders, and include stretches of fist-size stones and pebbles. Extend the rocks away from the pool in irregular widths to disguise the manufactured shape of the pool and give it a less uniform—and thus less attention-grabbing—outline. Intersperse the groups of rock with graceful clumps of ornamental grasses, and add perennials and a few shrubs. Sprinkle seeds of forget-me-not (*Myosotis sylvatica*) or monkey flower (*Mimulus* hybrids) among the stones, where they can form a casual splash of color. The plants around your pool resemble a smaller version of the edge habitat that birds find so appealing.

Wow, that water is cold! This Hermit Thrush proves that bathing birds can provide plenty of comical poses. Focus your binoculars on the bath to get a close-up view of the activity, or practice your action shots with a camera focused on your yard's water feature.

Avoid going overboard when adding water plants in your pool; they will spread quickly. Ask at a nursery for advice on plant selections. In general you'll want to include plants rooted in containers, such as water lilies; floating plants, such as water lettuce; and oxygenating plants, such as pondweed, which stay mostly submerged. If your pool is less than 2 feet deep and you live in an area with cold winters, keep water plants in pots so that you can lift and store them over winter. Keep the containers in tubs of water in a cool garage over the winter and set them out in the pool again in spring.

Insects attracted by water are a bonus to birds, which will make good use of them. Other wildlife, such as salamanders and frogs, will soon discover your garden pool.

A POOL TO ATTRACT WILDLIFE

Pebble beach
Gentle slope lets birds approach water gradually

Floating plants
Shade water and provide landing pads for insects

Trees and shrubs
Attract beneficial insects, provide food and cover for birds

Food for waterfowl
Include duckweed and duck potato

Grasses
Provide food and cover near water year-round

Rock nooks and crannies
Provide hiding places for insects and good foraging for birds

Bird-attracting marginal and bog plants
Provide food and nectar for a wide variety of birds

MUSICAL, MOVING WATER

Dripping, splashing, and gurgling water music is one of the best ways to attract birds. A bubbler in this stone fountain draws American Goldfinches and Pine Siskins to the sound of moving water.

The sound of gently moving water is extremely appealing to birds. In fact, bird banders often lure birds with dripping water. Audible water in the garden can be provided by a simple dripping hose or by a sophisticated waterfall that requires complex plumbing. However you supply it, remember that a little water music goes a long way. A thunderous waterfall or a huge, erupting fountain will frighten more birds than it attracts. Small drips, tinkles, and bubbles are what birds like.

A simple dripper can be made with a small-diameter clear plastic tube that runs up the trunk of a tree and out a low-hanging branch over the birdbath. An adapter will enable you to connect the tubing to the garden hose and disconnect it easily when you need the hose for other purposes. A shutoff clamp with an adjustable screw attached to the outflow end of the tube will allow precise regulation of the water flow.

Many birds love to fly through mist and fine sprays. Hang a hose with the nozzle set on mist spray over a tree branch or some other raised support. Or use a soaker hose that emits mist or fine streams of water. Turn the water on regularly at a set time of day, and birds will quickly learn when to expect this treat. Hummingbirds are very fond of bathing this way.

Fountains and waterfalls are as pleasing to people as they are to birds. Some birdbaths are equipped with fountains and jet sprays that bubble or spray up from the center of the pool. A simple waterfall can be constructed as a series of basins, with water falling from one to another. Whether you buy a kit or purchase the necessary hardware separately, make sure that the receiving basin at the bottom is deep enough to keep the pump out of sight and covered with water.

Natural-looking waterfalls and streams can add an exciting dimension to your yard or garden. However, they require some artistry and technical expertise to build. Many people consider hiring a professional landscape architect for this job. Remember, though, that shallow areas and a gentle flow of water are the keys to attracting birds.

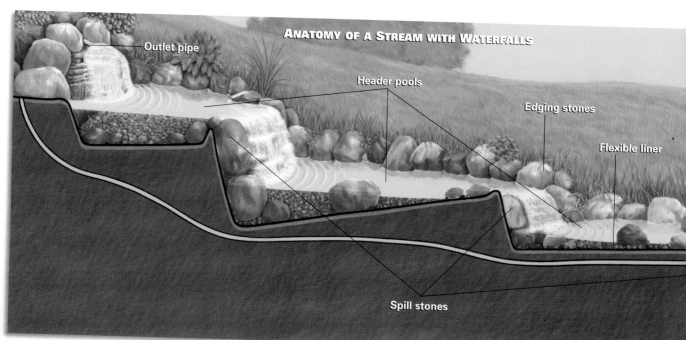

ANATOMY OF A STREAM WITH WATERFALLS

Outlet pipe

Header pools

Edging stones

Flexible liner

Spill stones

DO IT YOURSELF

If you want to build a waterfall yourself, keep it small and simple. An easy one is based on the same principle as the birdbath basin dug into the ground. On a sloping hillside, dig in a series of basins so that they overlap, one above the other, in stair-step fashion. Pay special attention to the angle and sharpness of each lip over which the water will flow. The idea is to prevent water from flowing or dripping back up under the basin, loosening soil and washing it into the system. The lip should be sharp and at a slight downward tilt so that water falls cleanly over the edge.

The bottom pool, or a hidden chamber adjacent to it, should be deep enough to hold a pump. Clear, flexible plastic tubing will return the water from the bottom basin back to the top. Hide the tubing by burying it in the ground or growing plants over it. The size of the pump you need will be determined by the intended rate of flow (which should be slow, for the birds' sake) and by how much higher the top basin is than the lowest one.

ELECTRICAL EXPERTISE

Consider carefully the placement of any birdbath, fountain, pool, or waterfall that requires electricity. Because your water feature is a permanent fixture, consider hiring an electrician, who can run a line out to it and install a switch inside the house. The safety and convenience of such a setup are well worth the expense. Such a line can also power lighting or the water heater you might use in winter to keep the water flowing.

Building your own waterfall is possible with just a few weekends of work, even if you're a beginner. Plan this permanent attraction carefully, and friends and family as well as birds and wildlife will enjoy it for years.

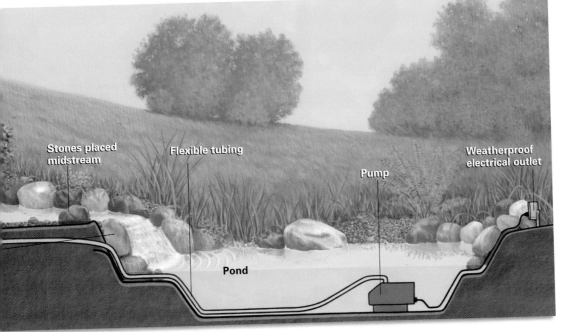

Stones placed midstream — Flexible tubing — Pump — Weatherproof electrical outlet — Pond

A stream is simply a series of garden pools running downhill over terraces.

PROVIDING HOUSING

The diminutive Eastern and Western Screech-Owls are the owls most likely to visit the garden. Only 7 to 10 inches tall, they may adopt a nest box in rural, suburban, or city backyards. These nocturnal hunters are a great aid in mouse control near feeders, but they may also nab an occasional backyard bird.

W hat a quiet, sad time spring would be without the music of birds. Proclaiming their territory and courting their mates, many of our favorite birds announce the start of their busiest season. Their elaborate territorial stakeouts and courtship rituals are only the beginning. Selecting a nesting site; collecting nesting materials and building a nest (which can take thousands of trips over a week or more); laying eggs and patiently incubating them; nurturing, feeding, warming, and protecting the helpless nestlings that emerge; and leading the infants to maturity—all these are jobs that will completely occupy the busy parents for the summer months.

Encourage birds to nest around your home by creating inviting habitat, as described in previous chapters. The most important thing to remember: Be patient. Birds may take a while—several seasons, even—to discover your efforts. Another avenue of attracting nesting birds is likely to have more immediate results: erecting birdhouses, also called nest boxes. Wrens, chickadees, bluebirds, nuthatches, titmice, and other birds that nest in cavities are often quick to adopt a birdhouse.

TERRITORIAL CONSIDERATIONS

Most birds are especially territorial during the breeding season, defending their chosen home grounds from intrusion by other birds of the same species. The size of a breeding territory varies with the species, from many square miles for some birds of prey to less than an acre for the American Robin. For some birds that nest in communities, such as the Purple Martin, the "territory," if it can be called that, may be only a few inches. The size of a territory can fluctuate from individual to individual within a species, depending on competition, population level, and available food and nesting sites. Some birds, such as the Northern Mockingbird, defend their territory with extraordinary zeal, attacking intruding birds and other creatures (including cats and humans) much larger than themselves.

Unless you live on property of estate dimensions, you will probably not attract more than one pair of each territorial species; each pair will drive away all competing individuals of its kind. Of course, your land may straddle a territorial boundary, and bird feeders may attract several pairs from adjacent territories. However, because different species prefer different feeding and nesting sites, they can and often do nest in surprising proximity, and it is quite possible to have a number of nesting pairs of different kinds of birds raising their young in the same small yard.

To increase the number of breeding pairs in your yard or garden, provide what this book has recommended throughout: diversity. The greater the number of types of plants, birdhouses, and nesting materials you provide, the greater the variety of nesting birds that will be drawn to your outdoor space. Six birdhouses for wrens, for example, built to the same style and dimensions, may draw only a single pair of wrens to your garden; the other five birdhouses will remain empty because the entrance hole or interior dimensions are too small to permit larger cavity nesters to use the box. Six birdhouses built to diverse specifications, however, and placed in appropriate habitat, may entice titmice, nuthatches, flickers, or even a screech-owl to join the nesting wrens in your yard.

This chapter describes the kinds of birdhouses, nesting shelves, and other shelters you can provide for birds in your home landscape, and presents ideas for supplying birds with nesting materials for use in birdhouses and other nests. For specific information on dimensions of birdhouses, including the diameter of entrances, see the chart on page 61.

Bluebirds, including the all-blue Mountain Bluebird of the West, are beloved birdhouse tenants.

The Baltimore Oriole weaves a sacklike nest that it hangs on the ends of drooping branches, high in a tree such as the American elm shown here. It readily uses a handout of short strings to build its nest.

NEST BOXES

American Kestrel

Mountain Chickadee

Tree Swallow house

Eastern Phoebe on nesting shelf

Eastern Bluebird pair

House Wren

About 50 species of North American birds are known to nest in birdhouses. (See page 61 for those most likely to use nest boxes around human dwellings.) Most of these birds naturally nest in cavities or crevices rather than constructing nests on tree limbs, in shrubs, or on the ground. In many areas the practice of clean forestry, agriculture, and gardening has severely reduced the availability of decaying trees that can be used as nesting sites. You can assist by supplying cavities in the form of birdhouses. A wide variety of commercially made birdhouses is available from hardware stores, garden centers, specialty bird stores, and mail-order firms. Some birdhouses are ready-made; others come in easy-to-assemble kits. Or you can make your own—an easy, inexpensive, and interesting project.

THE BASIC NEST BOX

The illustration at the top of page 61 presents a design for a birdhouse you can build yourself. This design is adaptable to accommodate nearly all cavity-nesting birds; consult the chart on page 61 for the dimensions appropriate to the species of bird you wish to attract. In building or buying a birdhouse, keep the following points in mind.

Pay careful attention to the diameter and placement of the entrance hole to exclude undesirable cavity-nesting birds (such as the House Sparrow and European Starling) from boxes designed for smaller birds. The diameter and placement of the entrance hole and the depth, width, and height of the interior (including available floor space) are important, but many species are close enough in their favored dimensions that the bird you get may not be the one you expected.

Birdhouses should be designed for a single nest. Except for the Purple Martin, a bird's territorial tendencies will prevent occupancy of more than one cavity.

In general the simplest, plainest design is most attractive to birds. Especially avoid birdhouses with parts that move in the wind or are made of highly reflective materials.

Well-seasoned wood ¾ inch to 1 inch thick is the best material for birdhouses, as it is weather-resistant and durable, breathes well, and is well-insulated to remain warm on cool days and cool on hot days. Redwood, white cedar, and cypress are extremely durable, but pine will also last a number of years. Avoid plastic, ceramic, or metal houses. Fasteners and hardware should be galvanized steel, brass, or other corrosion-resistant material.

Paint is unnecessary, but if you wish to paint the birdhouse, use latex paint. Do not paint the interior. Natural, dull colors, especially browns, grays, and greens, are best. White helps keep temperatures down in hot sun, and many species don't seem to mind it.

Plan ahead for how you intend to mount the box. The two most common ways are on top of a wooden post or sturdy wooden pole, or screwed to a wall, metal post, or tree trunk. A back piece that extends at least 2 inches beyond the sides or top provides a convenient surface through which to nail or screw the house to its support.

Mounting should be strong, secure, and stable. Loosely mounted boxes that can jiggle or sway in the wind or when a parent alights are not attractive to birds (except for wrens, which accept hanging houses). If a birdhouse presents even the slightest chance of coming loose and falling to the ground, it is a potential death trap.

DISCOURAGING STARLINGS AND HOUSE SPARROWS

Entrance holes 1½ inches or less in diameter will exclude starlings, but they need to be 1⅛ inches or less to exclude House Sparrows. Unfortunately, this size also excludes many desirable birds.

Another approach (requiring close observation) is to mount birdhouses just as the desired species is returning in spring.

To prevent competition from larger birds at a natural cavity, trace the hole and cut a disk of wood to fit. Drill a hole sized for smaller birds, and insert the barrier into the cavity, as shown.

DIMENSIONS FOR NEST BOXES AND NESTING SHELVES

Bird	Floor of House	Height of House	Diameter of Entrance Hole	Height of Entrance Above Floor	Height Above Ground
NEST BOXES					
Bluebirds	5×5"	8"	1½"	6"	4–5'
Chickadees	4×4"	8–10"	1⅛"	6–8"	6–15'
Flicker, Northern	7×7"	16–18"	2½"	14–16"	6–20'
Kestrel, American	8×8"	12–15"	3"	9–12"	10–30'
Martin*, Purple	6×6"	6"	2½"	1"	12–20'
Nuthatches	4×4"	8–10"	1¼"	6–8"	12–20'
Screech-Owls	8×8"	12–15"	3"	9–12"	10–30'
Swallow, Tree	5×5"	6"	1½"	1–5"	10–15'
Titmice	4×4"	8–10"	1¼"	6–8"	6–15'
Woodpecker, Downy	4×4"	8–10"	1¼"	6–8"	6–20'
Woodpecker, Hairy	8×8"	12–16"	1¾"	10–15"	5–30'
Woodpecker, Red-bellied	6×6"	12–15"	2½"	9–12"	12–20'
Woodpecker, Red-headed	6×6"	12–15"	2"	9–12"	12–20'
Wren, Carolina	4×4"	6–8"	1½"	4–6"	6–10'
Wren, House	4×4"	6–8"	1–1¼"	4–6"	6–10'
Wren, Winter	4×4"	6–8"	1–1¼"	4–6"	6–10'
NESTING SHELVES					
Phoebes	6×6"	6"			8–12'
Robin, American	6×8"	8"			6–15'
Sparrow, Song	6×6"	6"			1–3'
Swallow, Barn	6×6"	6"			8–12'

Dimensions are for one compartment (one pair of birds); Purple Martin houses are usually built eight compartments at a time.

CONSTRUCTION PLAN FOR BASIC NEST BOX

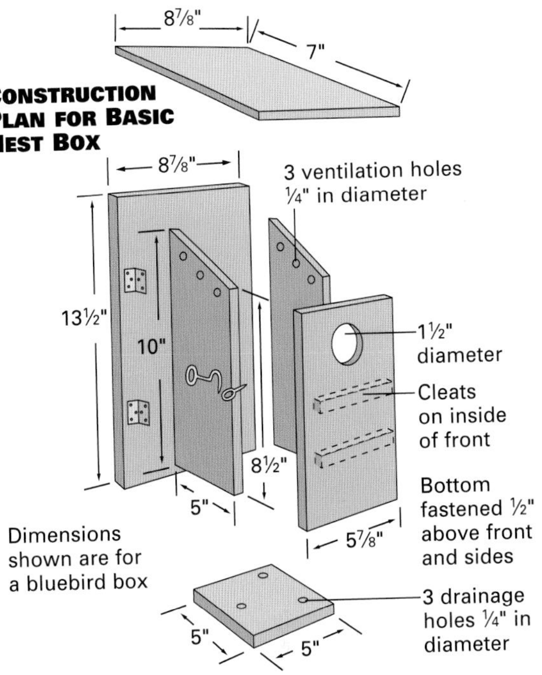

8⅞" · 7"

8⅞"

3 ventilation holes ¼" in diameter

13½"

10"

1½" diameter

Cleats on inside of front

8½"

5"

5⅞"

Bottom fastened ½" above front and sides

Dimensions shown are for a bluebird box

5" 5"

3 drainage holes ¼" in diameter

The roof of the nest box should be sloping and should overlap the front and sides by at least 1½". One inch back from the front edge of the roof, score a drip line ⅛" deep on the underside. Do not attach a perch on the outside. On the inside just below the entrance hole, attach two horizontal cleats (or score two horizontal cuts ⅛" deep) to assist nestlings when they fledge. Drill three ¼" holes for ventilation at the top of each side, placed above the level of the entrance in order to avoid drafts. One side of the nest box must be removable or hinged to permit removal of old nests and cleaning after the nestlings have left. However, the opening side must be able to be locked firmly in place while the box is in use. Unless drainage is otherwise provided, drill three ¼" holes into the bottom of the box.

NESTING SHELVES

Essentially, a nesting shelf is a birdhouse without sides or a front. The American Robin, Barn Swallow, Eastern and Black Phoebes, and rarely the Song Sparrow can be persuaded to use nesting shelves. Shelves should be mounted under eaves against the house, garage, or shed. In the case of American Robins, a vine-covered arbor is an attractive location. The illustration at right shows the basic design of a nesting shelf; the dimensions given in the chart above show the size of shelf that various species prefer.

A shelf for a Barn Swallow should be roofless, so it definitely needs the protection of an overhanging eave. Barn Swallows nest together in communities. They can be encouraged to nest on the side of a building by attaching 2×4s horizontally against a wall, and by providing an adequate supply of mud to use in building nests. The mud should be located in an open, unobstructed area.

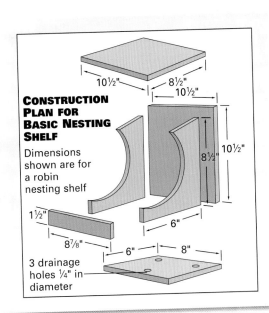

CONSTRUCTION PLAN FOR BASIC NESTING SHELF

Dimensions shown are for a robin nesting shelf

10½" 8½"

10½"

8½" 10½"

1½"

8⅞" 6" 8"

6" 6"

3 drainage holes ¼" in diameter

A SPECIAL HOUSE FOR PURPLE MARTINS

Superb aerialists, Purple Martins eat incredible numbers of flying insects and add a constant and delightful musical chatter to the neighborhood.

Along with its melodious calls, graceful flight, and diet of tens of thousands of flying insects, the interesting social behavior of the Purple Martin makes attracting this bird well worth the effort. The Purple Martin prefers nesting near human habitations in colonies. The best way to attract them is with a martin house.

Many excellent, affordable martin houses are available ready-made. Commercially made aluminum martin houses are lightweight, easy to put up and take down, and weather-resistant. Compared to wooden houses, they require less refinishing and maintenance. Extensive testing has resulted in houses designed to provide air circulation and exceptional heat-reflecting capacity.

If you are a confirmed do-it-yourselfer, and welcome the challenge of building your own multi-compartment martin house, you can find plans in books on birdhouse construction, or design your own, following the dimensions outlined on the chart on page 61.

Whether you buy or build one yourself, your martin house should meet important guidelines.

MARTIN HOUSE REQUIREMENTS

■ **CORRECT SIZE.** Each nesting compartment of the martin house should be built to the correct dimensions (see the chart on page 61).

■ **EXPANDABILITY.** Expandable houses allow you to add on as the colony grows. Some have more than 100 compartments, but it is best to start small, with eight to 12.

■ **WHITE COLOR.** White is the best color for a house. It reflects the heat of the sun and provides a sharp contrast with the dark entrance openings, making them more visible.

■ **GOOD VENTILATION.** Provide holes cut above the entrance of each compartment. A central air shaft that allows rising heat to escape through attic vents is also advisable.

■ **EASE OF CLEANING, MOUNTING, AND STORING.** A martin house should be cleaned annually, before the birds return in spring. Many aluminum houses feature a convenient pulley-and-winch apparatus that telescopes the pole. Store wooden houses under cover in winter.

■ **SUITABLE LOCATION.** If you don't have a suitable location for a martin house, there is little chance it will be used. A martin house should be mounted on a pole 12 to 20 feet high, on an open lawn or in a meadow at least 40 feet from any tree, structure, or other flight obstruction, but within 100 feet of a human dwelling (the Purple Martin seems to prefer nesting close to homes). Even shrubs or small trees more than 5 feet tall are a hindrance; these birds like to approach the nest in long, gliding swoops. Nearby bodies of water and large lawns and meadows are a plus, because martins need large, open areas to hunt insects on the wing. Utility wires about 30 yards from the martin house are another advantage—the birds use them as perches.

■ **PROTECTION FROM COMPETITION.** It is important that the martins be the first birds to stake a claim when housing is offered for the first time. If other hole-nesting birds are present, the martins will go elsewhere. Use plastic cups to block entrance holes. As soon as the martins arrive, remove the cups.

Long ago, gourds were used to house Purple Martins near Choctaw and Chickasaw dwellings, and in dooryards of the rural South, where the birds were believed to chase hawks away from poultry. Martins still find the gourds an inviting home.

HOUSING FOR BLUEBIRDS

Among the most sought-after birdhouse tenants throughout the country, the Mountain, Western, and Eastern Bluebirds are all in need of nesting sites. Since around 1900 the number of bluebirds has dropped sharply because of competition from European Starlings and House Sparrows for nest sites. At the same time, clean farming and forestry have deprived birds of the dead trees and rotting fence posts where they used to find cavities for nesting.

Bluebirds are making a remarkable comeback, thanks to thousands of birdhouses placed in yards and parks and along roads and highways throughout North America. Some landlords supervise hundreds of boxes, usually spaced at least 300 feet apart. (Always obtain the permission of the landowner before placing a birdhouse on his or her property.)

Bluebirds prefer nesting along the edge of pastures and cropland as well as in open residential areas, golf courses, and grassy parkland. Once bluebirds accept a house, they are likely to come back year after year. Houses that were used for nesting in early summer are often used for roosting at night later in the season, before migration.

Attach the house to a metal post or utility pole no higher than 5 feet from the ground. Keep the bluebird box as far from human habitations and activity as possible.

Bluebirds are strongly territorial and will constantly fight one another if their nests are too close together. Three nest boxes may be squeezed into a one-acre garden, however, if they are placed at least 300 feet apart and preferably away from and on opposite sides of the house, garage, or other large obstruction.

Your efforts make a difference, as this Eastern Bluebird pair confirms. To cavity-nesting bluebirds, every birdhouse counts.

DISCOURAGING COMPETITORS

For the proper dimensions of a bluebird house, see the chart on page 61. White, gray, brown, or green are suitable colors. The required 1½-inch entrance hole will exclude starlings but not House Sparrows.

If House Sparrows enter a house with bluebird eggs or young, they will promptly destroy whatever they find (even occasionally an adult). House Sparrows may be discouraged from nesting in a bluebird box by placing it at a low height, 4 to 5 feet from the ground. In general it is best to simply avoid placing bluebird houses near human dwellings where House Sparrows are abundant. Otherwise, you will have a constant and often losing battle to keep sparrows under control.

To discourage competition with wrens, place bluebird houses at least 40 to 50 feet away from the dense brushy cover and forest edge that are preferred wren habitat. Keep bluebird houses in as open an area as possible. As for other tenants—swallows, chickadees, titmice, nuthatches—treasure them as much as bluebirds. They also are in need of housing.

To facilitate inspection the house should be easy to open. While bluebirds are looking for nesting sites, inspect the boxes weekly. Remove House Sparrow nests if these interlopers are present, check for vandalism, and remove any wasp nests inside the box. A dusting of rotenone or sulfur when the house is unoccupied will discourage lice and other insect pests. After the young have left, remove the old nest and any infertile eggs to clear the way for subsequent broods. Bluebirds sometimes nest two or three times a season.

BEING A GOOD LANDLORD

You will have a better chance of attracting tenants if you plan the placement of birdhouses carefully and protect them from intrusions. It is tempting to frequently inspect a birdhouse to check for occupants, but too many close-up visits may disturb birds that are considering the house or nesting in it. Although birds will not desert a house that has human scent on it, your visits may alert predators to the nest. However, routine maintenance after nesting helps your birdhouses last longer and protects the birds from outbreaks of insect pests that could threaten the brood.

Provide squirrels with their own nest boxes so that they don't customize birdhouses by gnawing a bigger hole.

BIRDHOUSE PLACEMENT

In an outdoor space of less than an acre, erecting more than one birdhouse attractive to a particular species is usually a waste of effort, with a few exceptions. Tree Swallow boxes, mounted on posts in the open and near water, can be as close together as 30 feet. The highly territorial House Wren likes to have a wide choice of nesting sites. The male House Wren arrives before the female in spring and constructs as many as a dozen nests in his territory. He then courts a female by taking her around and showing off his work. When she finally accepts one of his nesting sites, a mating bond is formed. Frequently, the first thing she does is tear apart his hard work and start over. Because of this ritual, setting out four or more wren houses is a powerful attraction for one pair.

Old nesting material may harbor parasites; cleaning out the nest after fledging is generally recommended.

Some houses built for certain birds may be used by a different species if they are of the same size or smaller. To deter House Sparrows and wrens from taking bluebird houses, place the box in the open, a site favored by bluebirds. House Sparrows and House Wrens prefer to nest near buildings and hedgerows.

Put up your birdhouses by late summer or early fall. This allows newly built nest boxes to weather properly before they are occupied in early spring. And the extent of shade, an important factor to many birds, can be determined better before trees lose their leaves. Chickadees, titmice, bluebirds, and other species may use birdhouses for shelter on cold winter nights.

If you are unable to get your bird boxes up in early fall, mount them no later than mid-January in the mildest parts of the United States or as late as early March in the coldest areas. Follow these guidelines, and you will have a better chance of attracting cavity-nesting birds.

BIRDHOUSE MAINTENANCE

Cleaning birdhouses each time young birds have fledged is generally recommended in order to control parasite populations that can build up in old nest material. The houses of birds that are likely to start more than one brood per season may be cleaned out as soon as the young have fledged.

To clean a house, open the side and remove the nest and any debris that has collected. A paint scraper is handy for lifting out old nests and getting into the cracks. Dust the interior with rotenone to control louse or mite infestations. Check the boxes in early spring before the nesting season begins to remove old nests of birds, squirrels, mice, and wasps.

PROTECTION FROM PREDATORS

Put birdhouses where cats can't reach them. Because of the threat of predators, birds are cautious about choosing a house that is on the main trunk of a tree. It's also much more difficult for you to protect tree-mounted houses from predators. Protecting a post- or a pole-mounted house from climbing intruders is much easier. On wooden or metal posts use a cone-shaped squirrel guard of the type recommended for bird feeders.

A post- or pole-mounted birdhouse is also superior because many birds prefer a nest site in an open, sunny spot rather than dense shade. Near the edge of a wood, facing south over an open expanse, is an excellent location for many birds. Open, grassy areas with a few trees—for example, an abandoned orchard—are also attractive to many. Those birds that dwell in deep woods, however—some woodpeckers, nuthatches, and chickadees—prefer forested sites.

Whether the birdhouse or shelf is placed in a tree, on a post, under eaves, or in an arbor, there should be a clear, unobstructed flight path to the entrance hole. However, a tree or clothesline nearby is appreciated. Birds will use a perch from 5 to 15 feet away from the nest box or shelf as a point from which to survey for danger before the final approach.

PROVIDING NESTING MATERIALS

Provide suitable nesting materials to offer a powerful inducement for birds to nest in your yard or garden. A single nest often consists of a thousand or even several thousand pieces, each requiring an individual search-and-carry mission. Particularly in super-tidy areas—where every dead twig is pruned off and thrown away, and where every mown blade of grass or loose leaf is swept into a plastic bag—the lack of nesting materials can remove your outdoor area from consideration as a nest site.

String, hair, fur, and feathers, particularly white ones, are prized by many nesting birds. Collect soft, curled white feathers from the lawn around a nearby duck pond, or donate a handful from an old feather pillow to the cause. If you keep a horse or a dog, collect the combings or brushings, which will delight Chipping Sparrows and other birds. *Cut stringy materials into lengths no longer than 8 inches. Longer pieces have caused entanglement and even strangulation.*

Don't place materials directly in a birdhouse, which will make it look as though it is already occupied. The one exception to this rule is wood chips. A large number of birds prefer boxes with a 1- to 2-inch layer of wood chips or shavings in the bottom. And many species actually require such a layer of chips or shavings before they will accept a bird box, including the American Kestrel, Downy Woodpecker, Hairy Woodpecker, Northern Flicker, Red-bellied Woodpecker, Red-headed Woodpecker, and all screech-owls, nuthatches, chickadees, and titmice.

WELL-PLACED OFFERINGS

Offer nesting materials in concentrated, readily observable piles and stashes. By concentrating the offerings, you reduce the time it takes a bird to find things and build a nest. Place collections of twigs, dried grasses, and dead leaves beneath a sheltering shrub so birds can reach them without leaving protective cover.

Empty containers such as suet feeders and wire baskets hung from a branch or nailed to a tree are good ways to offer nesting materials; they are convenient for birds, and wind can't scatter the materials. Fill the containers with tufts of wool, dryer lint, lengths of string and yarn, horsehair, and other soft materials. A wire container is also a good holder for moss saved from floral arrangements; the Eastern Phoebe and chickadees are likely customers.

You can also offer soft materials by placing them in a conspicuous spot in the open, such

A wire suet feeder stuffed with string, yarn, and other fibers attracts nest-building birds, such as this Baltimore Oriole. Keep pieces of string and yarn short—no longer than 8 inches. White feathers from an old pillow are a real prize. Scatter a handful on the lawn and see who retrieves them.

as on the lawn or draped over a clothesline. Orioles are adept at retrieving lengths of white string draped over shrubs.

Several birds—including the American Robin, Wood Thrush, Eastern Phoebe, and Barn Swallow—require mud to construct their nests. Assist and encourage them to nest nearby by keeping a supply of mud handy during the nest-building season. Sink a garbage can lid into an open but unobtrusive place and keep it full of wet, sticky clay soil.

SUITABLE NESTING MATERIALS

String	Moss
Fur	Yarn
Human hair	Tufts of wool
Horsehair	Absorbent cotton
Dog and cat combings	Narrow cloth strips
	Thread
Feathers	Wood shavings

GALLERY OF BIRDS

Although the Northern Cardinal vigorously defends its territory against other cardinals during breeding season, winter feeders may host as many as a dozen pairs.

This chapter offers specific information for attracting 75 popular birds most likely to visit North American gardens. The description for each bird includes:

■ **A PHOTOGRAPH.** Unless otherwise noted, the example presented is a male in breeding plumage.

■ **A RANGE MAP.** The summer breeding range is shown in gold, the winter range in purple, and the permanent range in green. For an explanation of the range of a bird, please see page 12.

■ **HABITAT REQUIREMENTS.** In this section the natural habitats preferred by that species are specified, as well as how to accommodate those preferences in your garden with plants and water.

■ **NESTING BEHAVIOR.** Nesting habits in the wild are outlined, along with instructions for providing nest boxes, nesting shelves, nesting materials, and preferred nesting plants in your garden.

■ **FEEDING PREFERENCES.** Detailed here are the feeding habits and food preferences of each species, both in the wild and at the feeder, including the kinds of food to offer in winter and summer as well as the kinds of feeders that bird prefers to use.

This gallery explains how to attract favorite birds; it is not intended to be used as a field guide for identification. For identification details of the many different birds that visit your garden, purchase one of the excellent field guides available. Please see page 92 for recommendations.

To make this book most convenient to use alongside a field guide, birds are listed in the same way that reputable field guides list birds—in evolutionary order by family according to the American Ornithologists' Union Check-list of Birds. Both the common and scientific names are provided for easy reference. If you prefer an alphabetical listing to find a bird, use the index at the back of this book; boldface type tells you where that bird species is found in this gallery for quick, easy reference.

FALCO SPARVERIUS

American Kestrel

In prey and preferred habitat, this jay-size falcon is the daytime counterpart of nocturnal screech-owls. A nest box is the best way to attract it.

HABITAT: This is a bird of open country, especially parks, farmland, and plains studded with a few trees or giant cacti or adjacent to woods and wooded canyons. It frequently resides in open areas at the edges of cities, towns, and suburbs; highways and utility rights-of-way; and even in urban areas. A nesting pair may come to a garden if it resembles a woodland edge or borders on open pastures, fields, parkland, or prairie. Nesting territory often averages about 250 acres per pair.

NESTING: Does not build a nest but lays eggs in the cavities of tall trees and cacti, on the ledges of cliffs, in crevices and holes of buildings (especially under eaves and gables), and in nest boxes. It prefers abandoned flicker holes. Place bird box in a tree or tall cactus next to an open area, 10 to 30 feet above the ground.

FEEDING: Feeds primarily on large insects (mainly grasshoppers) and small rodents but occasionally eats small songbirds. The prolific House Sparrow is among its favorite prey. In arid climates it is able to extract all the water it needs from its food.

The American Kestrel is the only North American falcon that uses nest boxes.

CALLIPEPLA CALIFORNICA

California Quail

This is a fast runner that flies only when it must. Winter coveys number up to 60 individuals. It is nonmigratory.

HABITAT: This sociable bird is found in open country where low trees and shrubs are broken by patches of grass and herbaceous plants, nearly always close to water. In the garden, dense, shrubby cover, flower borders, and a source of water on the ground are attractive. Roosts in low trees 15 to 25 feet high.

NESTING: The nest is usually a shallow, grass-lined scrape in the ground in a clump of tall grasses and weeds, under a shrub or brush pile, or in the open next to a rock or log. Occasionally it nests up to 10 feet off the ground in a tree or vine. It readily nests in gardens, often next to much-used paths near the house. Flowerbeds, hedges, and clumps of cacti are favorite nesting spots.

FEEDING: The California Quail is habitual in its feeding, returning daily if food is abundant. It feeds almost entirely on the ground or in low branches of shrubs. Bush clover is a favorite food shrub. Attract quail by scattering corn and mixed birdseed on the ground.

The California Quail often nests in western gardens. The male and female raise each brood together.

COLUMBA FASCIATA

Band-tailed Pigeon

This shy forest bird is becoming common in cities, parks, and gardens in the West. It winters in the Southwest and tropical America.

HABITAT: Coniferous forests along the West Coast, and oak and oak-pine woodlands in the interior are the haunts of this relative of the common pigeon. It tends to roost in large flocks and nest high in trees, coming down to forage in grass and low shrubs. Gardens that combine tall conifers (especially redwood and fir), large deciduous trees (especially oaks, sycamore and alder), lawn, and shrubs are often visited. Food plants include oak, pine, grape, elderberry, cherry, chokecherry, mulberry, manzanita, dogwood, salal, blueberry, juniper, and holly. A source of water is essential.

NESTING: Constructs a loose platform of sticks and twigs in a tree (usually fir, spruce, oak, or alder) or shrub 10 to 40 feet above the ground. Often nests in scattered pairs, more rarely in larger groups.

FEEDING: Feeds on many insects in summer, especially grasshoppers. Acorns (swallowed whole) are its primary plant food, along with many berries and seeds. Offer scratch feed, cracked corn, and mixed birdseed on the ground or on low platform feeders.

The Band-tailed Pigeon prefers gardens with a reliable source of water near the ground.

ZENAIDA MACROURA

Mourning Dove

Mourning Doves often visit ground feeders every morning and evening as regularly as clockwork.

This gregarious bird is a regular visitor to many winter feeding stations, often in flocks of up to 20 individuals. In summer it often nests in gardens. **HABITAT:** Open land with scattered trees and shrubs is preferred, although this adaptable bird thrives in habitats as diverse as eastern woodlands, midwestern plains, and western mesquite deserts and scrub. It frequently visits water for drinking and bathing. The best garden habitats include open lawn, herbaceous borders and flowerbeds with scattered trees and shrubs, and a source of water on the ground.

NESTING: The Mourning Dove frequently nests in gardens, especially if food and water are convenient and abundant. The nest is a loose platform constructed 5 to 25 feet above the ground, often in the crotch of a shrub or tree but also in vines, gutters, or chimneys. **FEEDING:** Sweet gum, alder, hollies, elders, spruces, and serviceberries are favorite garden plants for food. It prefers to eat at ground feeders and on the ground under raised feeders. White and red proso millet, oil-type sunflower seed, and canary seed are favorite foods, along with black-striped and hulled sunflower seed, milo, corn, buckwheat, and wheat.

Because screech-owls eat rodents and insects, they are a valuable asset to the garden.

O. KENNICOTTII, OTUS ASIO

Screech-Owls

These small owls rest quietly in trees during the day and become active at night. They often nest around gardens. The Eastern Screech-Owl is native east of the Rocky Mountains, the Western Screech-Owl in the West. **HABITAT:** Resides in open woods, woodland edges bordering open fields, and old fields with scattered trees and shrubs. In the Southwest they inhabit deserts with giant saguaro cacti, wooded canyons, and

wooded streams and lakeshores. In gardens they prefer dense stands of trees with adjoining open areas for hunting, and a source of water for nocturnal drinking and bathing. **NESTING:** Screech-owls lay their eggs in the cavities of trees, stumps, and saguaro cacti, often in abandoned flicker holes. They will nest in a bird box of the right size mounted in a tree 10 to 30 feet above the ground. Screech-owls compete with flickers, American Kestrels, and squirrels for nesting sites. Nest boxes are also useful as roosting boxes in winter. **FEEDING:** Feed chiefly on large insects, small rodents, and, more rarely, small reptiles and songbirds.

ARCHILOCHUS COLUBRIS

Ruby-throated Hummingbird

The pugnacious Ruby-throated Hummingbird will drive off birds as large as hawks and crows.

This is the only hummingbird that breeds in the eastern United States and the only one likely to be found there. **HABITAT:** In the wild this is a bird mostly of woodland edges and openings, especially near brooks and streams where its favorite nectar plants grow. Many gardens are ideal habitats, especially those with a margin of trees and shrubby borders surrounding a central lawn, with herbaceous borders and flowerbeds. It has a strong preference for red, pink, or orange tubular flowers. Many garden plants are important sources of nectar, especially red

columbine, scarlet sage, trumpet honeysuckle, petunia, phlox, bee balm, and trumpet creeper. Running water, especially a gentle, trickling waterfall or a misty spray, is appreciated. **NESTING:** Constructs a tiny cup nest on the saddle of a horizontal or downsloping twig or limb of a tree, 5 to 25 feet above the ground, often overhanging a stream. **FEEDING:** Flower nectar is the chief food of the Ruby-throated Hummingbird, but it also eats tiny insects and spiders. It readily visits hummingbird feeders stocked with sugar water. For more information on attracting and feeding hummingbirds, see pages 28 and 29.

CALYPTE ANNA

Anna's Hummingbird

This hummingbird is the only one that winters around its home range in the United States (mostly California). It is the most common garden hummingbird in California.

HABITAT: Chaparral and woodlands at the margins of rivers and streams are favored, especially where live oak and scrub oak predominate. Garden habitats include shrub borders and woodland edges heavy with suitable nectar plants such as eucalyptus, tree tobacco, century plant, and fuchsia.

NESTING: Anna's Hummingbird constructs a tiny cup nest of plant down, spider silk, and bits of lichen and moss on the saddle of a horizontal limb or twig in a shrub or low tree, in semishade. The nest is so small and cleverly camouflaged that it is rarely noticed.

FEEDING: Although it feeds largely on flower nectar, Anna's Hummingbird eats more tiny insects and spiders than do most other hummingbirds. It will also feed on sap from damaged trees and the holes left in trees by sapsuckers. Anna's Hummingbird comes readily to hummingbird feeders. For more information on attracting hummingbirds, see pages 28 and 29.

Sage blossoms are attractive sources of nectar for Anna's Hummingbird.

CALYPTE COSTAE

Costa's Hummingbird

Of all North American hummingbirds, Costa's Hummingbird is best adapted to desert conditions.

HABITAT: Less dependent on water than other North American hummingbirds, this bird inhabits low-elevation desert in the Southwest, and desert and dry chaparral in California. It seems well-adapted to irrigated gardens, especially in Southern California, where it may be a permanent resident. Among its favorite garden flowers are yucca, red penstemon, lemon bottlebrush, chuparosa, coral bells, Mexican sage, ocotillo, scarlet larkspur, and tree tobacco.

NESTING: Constructs a tiny, loose cup nest of willow or yucca down, feathers, dry leaves, lichen, and sometimes bits of paper, held together with spider silk. Often built in dead yucca plants, nests can also be found on cactus branches and limbs or twigs of sage, palo verde, willows, and alder.

FEEDING: Like all hummingbirds it feeds on nectar, small insects, and spiders. Because of its shorter bill, it is more limited than others to flowers with a shorter tube. It comes readily to hummingbird feeders. For more information on attracting hummingbirds, see pages 28 and 29.

Yucca and red penstemon are important plants throughout the range of the Costa's Hummingbird.

SELASPHORUS RUFUS

Rufous Hummingbird

Wintering in Mexico and breeding in Alaska and the Pacific Northwest, this hummingbird is most often observed in gardens during its springtime flight northward through the valleys of California, Oregon, and Washington or on its late-summer flight south through the mountains.

HABITAT: Breeds in mountain meadows and lowland forest edges and woodland openings, especially near running water. Best garden habitats resemble woodland edges and openings, with a margin of trees and shrubby borders surrounding open lawn and flowerbeds. Favorite nectar plants include crimson-flowered currant, red columbine, fuchsia, geranium, jasmine, trumpet vine, citrus, penstemon, tiger lily, Indian paintbrush, madrone, and manzanita. Rock gardens with alpine flowers make it feel at home.

NESTING: Builds a typical tiny cup nest of plant down, spider silk, and lichen on the branch or twig of a conifer.

FEEDING: Like all hummingbirds it is strongly attracted to red flowers and will investigate nearly any bright red object. It often visits hummingbird feeders. For more information on attracting hummingbirds, see pages 28 and 29.

The Rufous Hummingbird cannot resist red and orange flowers, such as this Indian paintbrush.

The Red-headed Woodpecker is fond of storing large amounts of food it may never use.

MELANERPES ERYTHROCEPHALUS

Red-headed Woodpecker

Because of competition with starlings for nest sites, this bird is increasingly rare. **HABITAT:** In the wild it is found in open land with scattered trees or shrubs, in logged-over or burned areas of deciduous forests, and in woods following rivers and streams. Gardens with widely spaced trees, a large dead tree, and an orchard nearby are attractive. Oak, beech, dogwood, serviceberry, tupelo, mountain ash, mulberry, and elderberry are favorite food plants. **NESTING:** Excavates a cavity in the stump or large branch of a dead or dying deciduous tree that is in the open but near a grove of other large trees. It may excavate a cavity in a utility pole or fence post or even under the eaves of a house. Use of nest boxes is rare. **FEEDING:** Forages for insects on the bark of tree trunks and for insects, fruit, and nuts (especially acorns) on the ground or in shrubs. At the winter feeder, it enjoys suet, sunflower seed, cracked corn, raisins, nutmeats, and baked goods.

The Red-bellied Woodpecker is the most frequently seen woodpecker at feeding stations in the Southeast.

MELANERPES CAROLINUS

Red-bellied Woodpecker

Like the Red-headed Woodpecker, this bird stores huge quantities of food to which it may not return. **HABITAT:** Deep to moderately open bottomland woods, especially swamp and floodplain woods along rivers and streams, are home to this bird. It is also common in oak, pine, and mixed coniferous-deciduous woods. It is a frequent resident in gardens with large, old trees, especially in the Southeast. Maple, pine, willow, and elm are favorite nesting trees. Important food plants include oak, beech, hickory, tupelo, dogwood, pine, elderberry, grape, cherry, mulberry, Virginia creeper, poison ivy, bayberry, and palmetto. **NESTING:** Excavates cavity in the trunk or stump of a dead or dying tree. Often uses nest boxes. **FEEDING:** Drills into trees for beetles and insect larvae and forages for insects and plant food on the ground and in shrubs. At the winter feeder, it eats suet, peanut butter mix, nutmeats, cracked corn, and sunflower seed. Fruit is often taken in spring and summer.

The Yellow-bellied Sapsucker drills sap wells in a checkerboard pattern of horizontal rows. The holes are seldom damaging to trees.

SPHYRAPICUS VARIUS

Yellow-bellied Sapsucker

Sapsuckers are the only woodpeckers known to use sap as a major food. Their sap wells are used by many birds and mammals. **HABITAT:** Sapsuckers are found in mixed coniferous-deciduous forests, especially near openings, logged-over groves of small deciduous trees, and wooded river bottoms and streamsides. Sapsuckers tend to breed in northern or mountainous areas where stands of aspen are common. **NESTING:** Sapsuckers nest and raise their young in cavities they excavate in live aspen, birch, spruce, or cottonwood trees. They frequently start several nesting holes before completing one. **FEEDING:** Sapsuckers return to the same sap wells many times. They also eat many insects and larvae and the fruits of holly, wild cherry, dogwood, Virginia creeper, red cedar, hackberry, elderberry, grape, and sassafras. At winter feeders they are partial to suet, peanut butter mix, and baked goods; in summer they will take grape jelly and sugar water from hummingbird feeders.

PICOIDES PUBESCENS

Downy Woodpecker

The most common woodpecker to visit winter feeders throughout most of the United States.

HABITAT: This woodpecker lives in open woodlands broken up by logged patches, old fields, and bodies of water, as well as deeper mixed coniferous-deciduous forests. Attractive gardens combine conifers and deciduous trees with shrubs and groves of young deciduous trees.

NESTING: Lays eggs in a cavity it excavates in a dead tree, stub, or stump from 5 to 50 feet above the ground. Prefers older nesting trees, such as birches, poplars, aspens, and elms, surrounded by a thicket of younger offspring. Will sometimes use a nest box of appropriate size.
FEEDING: Feeds chiefly on insects that it chips out while clinging to the bark of a tree trunk. Plant foods include dogwood, serviceberry, Virginia creeper, tupelo, apple, hornbeam, sumac, oak, beech, and walnut. At winter feeders it is especially attracted by suet, peanut butter mix, and nutmeats. It also eats baked goods, especially corn bread, and cracked corn.

The size of a House Sparrow, the Downy Woodpecker is the smallest woodpecker in North America.

PICOIDES VILLOSUS

Hairy Woodpecker

This robin-size woodpecker looks like a large version of the Downy Woodpecker, although it is a bit more shy.
HABITAT: The Hairy Woodpecker breeds in deciduous forests, then moves into more open areas of scattered trees and orchards in winter. Gardens with many older deciduous trees at least 8 inches in diameter are especially appealing.

NESTING: Excavates cavity in a live deciduous tree (usually aspen in the North, oak in the South, but also maple, apple, and beech). May use a nest box of appropriate size, mounted 5 to 30 feet above ground on the trunk of a deciduous tree and lined with a bed of wood chips.
FEEDING: About 75 percent of this bird's diet consists of insects, mostly woodborers but also beetles, ants, and spiders gleaned from trunks of trees. Bramble berries, acorns, hazelnuts, and beechnuts are important plant foods, as well as sap from sapsucker wells. Will come to feeders for suet, sunflower seed, nutmeats, peanut butter, and chopped fresh fruit.

In the wild the Hairy Woodpecker eats sap from sapsucker wells. In the garden it sometimes takes nectar from hummingbird feeders.

COLAPTES AURATUS

Northern Flicker

The Yellow-shafted, Gilded, and Red-shafted Flickers are now known to be subspecies of the Northern Flicker.
HABITAT: Flickers are found in open woods, old fields with scattered shrubs and open groves, as well as woods following the course of rivers and streams, desert washes, and deserts with saguaro cactus. Gardens with a mix of coniferous and deciduous trees, open grassy and shrubby areas, and groves of young

deciduous trees are most appealing. Because flickers use lawns to forage for ants, open ground is a necessity.
NESTING: Flickers nest in cavities they excavate in the trunks or stubs of old dead trees, almost always surrounded by shrubs or saplings. They may also nest in utility poles, fence posts, the sides of barns and other buildings, and saguaro cactus. They readily use nest boxes built to the appropriate dimensions, mounted on a tall post over a dense planting of shrubs and small trees and well filled with fine wood shavings or coarse sawdust.
FEEDING: In summer Flickers eat an enormous number of ants, as well as other insects. They often visit the

winter feeder, where they eat suet, peanut butter mix, nutmeats, and baked goods.

The Northern Flicker favors old dead apple, elm, cottonwood, sycamore, oak, and pine trees for nesting.

SAYORNIS NIGRICANS

Black Phoebe

The Black Phoebe may reside in southwestern gardens if a lake, pond, or stream is nearby.

Where this southwestern flycatcher inhabits valleys and coastal areas, it is generally a year-round resident. In harsher climates, especially at higher altitudes, it may migrate south for the winter. It can be distinguished from the Dark-eyed Junco by its thin, flat bill adapted to catching insects, its upright posture, and its habit of tail-wagging.

HABITAT: The Black Phoebe is partial to waterside habitats, especially brooks, ponds, lakes, irrigation ditches, and canals under a canopy of trees. Garden pools, ponds, and streams, with their accompanying lush vegetation, are most attractive to this bird.

NESTING: The Black Phoebe attaches a mud nest mixed with twigs, grasses, and other fibrous plant materials to the rough wall of a cliff or bluff. Unlike that of the Eastern Phoebe, the nest is not supported on a ledge or shelf. The Black Phoebe frequently nests on human structures, such as under eaves or bridges, or inside wells. It breeds from March to August.

FEEDING: These birds are insectivorous, darting down from a low perch in the branches of a tree, or a wall or fence, to snap up flying or crawling insects close to the ground, lawn, or surface of a pond.

SAYORNIS PHOEBE

Eastern Phoebe

Unlikely to visit feeding stations, the Eastern Phoebe often nests in gardens, especially near water.

The Eastern Phoebe has adapted its breeding habitat to favor human structures that are near running water (especially bridges).

HABITAT: The Eastern Phoebe prefers waterside habitats, especially wooded streamsides that are near bridges crossing streams or that are flanked by rocky ravines. It is attracted by sizable garden streams, pools with waterfalls, and other sources of running water. Sumac, wax myrtle, holly, hackberry, blueberry, cherry, elderberry, and sassafras are important food plants in its winter range.

NESTING: The Eastern Phoebe builds its nest on ledges and in crevices of rocky walls of cliffs and ravines, or in caves. It often nests on structures, such as under eaves, on the rafters of attics, sheds, and barns, on windowsills, and most frequently on girders underneath bridges crossing streams. It often returns several years in a row to the same nesting spot. It will use a special nesting shelf built to the correct specifications and mounted under the eaves of a house or porch near a suitable streamside habitat.

FEEDING: The Eastern Phoebe is almost entirely insectivorous in spring, summer, and early fall but is fond of fruits and berries in winter.

CYANOCITTA STELLERI

Steller's Jay

Shy in forest breeding grounds, the Steller's Jay is famously bold around campgrounds and winter feeders.

A familiar sight in campgrounds and parks, the Steller's Jay is the western counterpart of the eastern Blue Jay in temperament and behavior.

HABITAT: This is mostly a bird of deep coniferous forests, including those of higher elevations, but it also inhabits mixed coniferous-deciduous forests. In fall and winter, it frequently moves into the more open oak woods of lowlands and even into the open woodlands of the western prairie states. Western gardens with many large conifers and oaks, particularly those near forests, are attractive to this jay.

NESTING: Builds a neat but bulky nest of sticks and twigs cemented together with mud and lined with grasses and fine plant rootlets. The nest is usually built on a forked branch of a dense, shady conifer.

FEEDING: This bird feeds from the high treetops to the ground. Most of its diet is vegetable, but it also eats insects (mostly bees and wasps) and sometimes plunders the nests of songbirds for eggs and young. Its most important food is acorns, but pine seeds, grains, and many fruits and berries are also eaten. It frequently visits feeders well stocked with peanuts, sunflower seed, suet, nutmeats, and finely cracked corn.

CYANOCITTA CRISTATA

Blue Jay

Amusing for its raucous and mischievous behavior, the Blue Jay can dominate feeders, driving off other birds.

HABITAT: Originally a cautious bird of deep forests dominated by oaks, the Blue Jay has been common in rural and suburban gardens and parks only since the first part of the 20th century. It prefers gardens with many older trees, especially oaks, beeches, and pines. A source of water is a major attraction.

NESTING: The Blue Jay's nest is a bulky cup of twigs and other plant materials, lined with grass and fine rootlets. It is built in the crotch of a tree or shrub, usually in a woodland of oaks and beeches but sometimes in a conifer near a house.

FEEDING: During winter and fall, acorns are the most important food, followed by beechnuts and waste corn. Other nuts, many seeds and fruits, and most berries are also attractive. In spring and summer, Blue Jays eat many insects and some small animals, including the eggs and young of birds. Common at winter ground and platform feeders, they are fond of whole peanuts and sunflower seed. Black- and gray-striped sunflower seed are much preferred over the black-oil type. Suet and nutmeats are also eaten. Corn is only moderately attractive.

Like crows, Blue Jays sound the alarm against predators for the whole bird community.

APHELOCOMA CALIFORNICA

Western Scrub-Jay

A little more shy at first than the eastern Blue Jay, this crestless bird quickly gets used to humans and displays its raucous personality.

HABITAT: Oak woodlands and chaparral are the haunts of the Western Scrub-Jay. It avoids low chaparral and scrub, where surveillance perches are more difficult to find. It is a frequent visitor and breeding resident of western gardens, particularly where dense shrubs and oaks predominate.

NESTING: In shrubs or low trees, this bird builds bulky nests made of sticks and twigs lined with grasses and fine plant rootlets.

FEEDING: Feeds almost entirely on the ground and occasionally in the low branches of a shrub. Its diet consists of nuts (especially acorns and pinyon seeds), many fruits and berries, and waste grain, supplemented in spring and summer with a wide variety of insects and small animals (including the eggs and young of birds). It is a frequent but cautious visitor to feeders for peanuts, nutmeats, sunflower seed, finely cracked corn, and crumbs of baked goods.

Although the Western Scrub-Jay feeds on or near the ground, it needs higher perches for lookout duty.

PROGNE SUBIS

Purple Martin

After wintering in South America, this swallow often returns to the same breeding spot year after year.

HABITAT: This aerial acrobat needs plenty of room. Grassy, open streamsides, river bottomlands and marshes, and meadows and large forest openings close to lakes and ponds are favored habitats. The best gardens include open lawns and meadows near large bodies of water, with trees in the distance.

NESTING: Historically this bird nested in crevices in the sides of bluffs and in natural cavities and woodpecker holes in hollow stumps (saguaro cactus in the Southwest). In the West these are still the preferred nesting sites. In the East it has learned to nest in gourds and apartment houses in communities of eight or more pairs. Such birdhouses are the only means of attracting this bird. See page 62 for more information on martin houses.

FEEDING: This bird consumes vast numbers of dragonflies, bees, and large beetles on the wing; and will sometimes come to a dish of mealworms. It will accept crumbled eggshells spread on the ground below an occupied house during nesting season.

The Purple Martin is best known for nesting in "apartment houses."

TACHYCINETA BICOLOR
Tree Swallow

Tree Swallows frequently nest in birdhouses placed on posts or trees that jut out of a body of water.

This graceful aerial enthusiast readily nests in birdhouses, especially in gardens that are close to water.

HABITAT: The Tree Swallow lives in a wide variety of waterside habitats, including wet meadows, marshes, swamps, and on the shores of lakes, ponds, and streams. Open lawns near water with a place to perch nearby (such as overhead wires) are important.

NESTING: Nests in natural cavities and abandoned woodpecker holes in tree stumps. White or pale gray feathers, such as chicken feathers, are favorite nesting materials, along with grasses and straw. The nest is always located close to a body of water, preferably a stump jutting directly out of water or overhanging it. Tree Swallows also nest in boxes built to the appropriate dimensions. They are one of the few birds that will tolerate several close neighbors of their own species; nest boxes can even be placed in the same tree.

FEEDING: Although they mostly eat insects caught on the wing, these swallows also feed on some berries and seeds. Fruits of bayberry and wax myrtle are especially favored; also berries of red cedar, autumn olive, Virginia creeper, and dogwood, and the seeds of bulrushes, sedges, and smartweed.

Most Violet-green Swallows overwinter in Mexico and Central America, although some remain year-round in Southern California.

TACHYCINETA THALASSINA
Violet-green Swallow

This familiar western bird is often seen perching in large flocks evenly spaced along overhead wires.

HABITAT: Widespread in forests, mountains, wooded foothills, or wherever dead trees can be found near water. It feeds over large fields and lawns as well as over ponds, lakes, and streams. It is often found in suburban areas and near towns.

NESTING: Constructs nest of grasses, plant stems, and feathers in abandoned woodpecker holes and other cavities in trees, outcrops, or rocky cliffs or sometimes under the eaves of a building. Offering chicken feathers is a real attraction; it has been known to take them directly from human hands. It will readily nest in bird boxes of appropriate size, mounted on a post near water. This bird is quite social, sometimes nesting in colonies of up to 20 pairs in a single dead standing tree in or near water.

FEEDING: Apparently this swallow feeds entirely on insects caught while flying. It is not known to visit bird feeders.

HIRUNDO RUSTICA
Barn Swallow

Although they drink and bathe on the wing, Barn Swallows alight on the ground to gather the mud essential for nest-building.

Some people consider swallows nesting on the walls of buildings a nuisance, but many more admire the spectacular grace of these birds in flight and appreciate their consumption of enormous quantities of flying insects. They winter in South America, as far south as Argentina.

HABITAT: Barn Swallows can be found in nearly any open country, often but not always close to water. Meadows, golf courses, parks, large lawns, pastures, and agricultural fields are favorite haunts. The best garden habitats for swallows include open lawns close to bodies of water.

NESTING: Originally the Barn Swallow adhered its nests to holes and crevices in the sides of caves, cliffs, and streambanks, but now it nests chiefly on human structures, such as under the eaves of barns and other farm outbuildings, and on houses, bridges, and other buildings. Attaching a horizontal 2×4 with its narrow side against a building will help encourage the Barn Swallow to nest. It will readily accept an offering of white, curly duck feathers scattered in an open area.

FEEDING: Barn Swallows feed exclusively on insects they catch while flying.

POECILE ATRICAPILLUS

Black-capped Chickadee

This jaunty, ever-curious bird is a frequent visitor to many gardens in winter. The nearly identical Carolina Chickadee is the counterpart species found in the southeastern United States.

HABITAT: Ranges through mixed forests of conifers and deciduous trees, isolated groves, and thickets of deciduous shrubs at edges and openings of coniferous forests.

Gardens should include dense shrub and sapling thickets backed by large deciduous and coniferous trees.
NESTING: Moves from forest edges and openings to dense woods for nesting. Sometimes it uses existing tree cavities, but often it digs its own hole out of partly rotted tree trunks or stumps, usually birch or pine. It readily uses bird boxes that are the correct size and lined with wood chips. Mount the box in dense woods on the rotting snag of a pine, birch, aspen, or elm tree.
FEEDING: Largely an insect eater in summer, at winter feeders it prefers oil-type sunflower seed, followed by black-striped, then gray-striped sunflower seed. Peanut kernels and other nutmeats, hulled sunflower seed, peanut butter mix, and suet are also eaten. Wobbly hanging feeders that few other birds can use are preferred.

Many other birds take advantage of the Black-capped Chickadee's keen ability to spot food and predators.

POECILE GAMBELI

Mountain Chickadee

This western high-country bird is most likely to be seen at the feeder in winter, when it descends to the more populated lower elevations in flocks sometimes accompanied by migrating warblers and vireos.

HABITAT: During breeding season this bird lives in the deep coniferous forests of inland mountain ranges dominated by pines, spruces, and firs, as well as high-elevation juniper woodlands. In fall and winter, it descends to oak woodlands in the foothills and to cottonwoods and willows along valley streams. It often forages in oaks, cedars, and pines when at lower elevations.

NESTING: Nest is constructed of soft plant materials, rabbit and squirrel fur, and cattle hair, often in natural cavities or abandoned woodpecker holes in trees but sometimes in a hole that the bird digs out of the soft wood of a rotting stump. Sometimes it will nest in a box of appropriate size.
FEEDING: Like the Black-capped Chickadee, the Mountain Chickadee is primarily an insect eater in summer. In fall and winter it accepts sunflower seed, nutmeats, peanut butter mix, and suet and seems to prefer hanging feeders.

Western gardens with plenty of conifers and oaks are most likely to attract the Mountain Chickadee.

POECILE RUFESCENS

Chestnut-backed Chickadee

This common bird of the forested Northwest is as inquisitive and sharp at spotting food as are its eastern relatives.

HABITAT: Inhabits moist, coniferous forests, especially the rain forests of the Pacific coast as well as interior woods along streams. Tall trees and dark woodlands, from dense conifers to eucalyptus, are key to attracting this bird.

NESTING: The Chestnut-backed Chickadee nests in natural cavities, in abandoned woodpecker holes, or in holes it digs out of rotting trees, usually firs. It often uses nest boxes.
FEEDING: Like other chickadees, this bird is mostly insectivorous in summer but readily eats seeds and berries in fall and winter. Pine seeds are its most important natural plant food, followed by poison oak berries, thimbleberries, and Pacific wax myrtle. At the feeding station, sunflower seed and suet are its favorite foods, but it will sometimes eat finely cracked corn and apples. Where the range of this bird overlaps that of the Black-capped Chickadee, it confines itself to foraging in tall trees, usually conifers, whereas the Black-capped Chickadee generally feeds lower in streamside thickets or oaks.

Like all chickadees, the Chestnut-backed Chickadee flies in winter flocks accompanied by other birds.

BAEOLOPHUS INORNATUS

Oak Titmouse

The Oak Titmouse is often a resident of western gardens year-round.

The Oak Titmouse displays the same vivacious behavior as its eastern relation, the Tufted Titmouse. It is a permanent resident throughout its range.

HABITAT: This bird prefers oak, pinyon, and juniper woodlands and deciduous woods, thickets, and shrubland with scattered trees. Streamsides and forest edges are especially attractive. It is adaptable to a wide variety of gardens.

NESTING: Nests in tree cavities, sometimes in natural holes and those abandoned by woodpeckers, and sometimes in holes it excavates itself in a rotting trunk or stump. Fence post holes, cavities in old buildings, and nest boxes of the correct dimensions are sometimes chosen. Attract breeding birds by setting out hair, bits of fur, feathers, and thread for nest-building.

FEEDING: The Oak Titmouse feeds mostly by clinging to twigs and limbs of trees and shrubs, but also forages on the ground. It is mostly insectivorous in spring and summer, and mostly vegetarian in winter. Important plant foods include acorns, cherries, pine seeds, walnuts, apples, thistle, and oats. At the feeder its tastes are similar to those of the Tufted Titmouse: peanut kernels, sunflower seed, suet, and peanut butter.

BAEOLOPHUS BICOLOR

Tufted Titmouse

The Tufted Titmouse treasures hair for nesting and has been known to pluck it from human heads!

This frequent visitor to the winter feeder is welcome for its jaunty disposition. It is a permanent resident.

HABITAT: Breeds and lives most of its life in deciduous woods in bottomlands, swamps, and riversides. It is most common in gardens in winter but may reside there all year if a dense cover of deciduous trees is available.

NESTING: Nests in the natural cavities of trees and abandoned woodpecker holes and will often use a nest box built to the proper dimensions. Place the nest box on a tree trunk or on a fence post in semishade. Placing hair (horsehair, combings from pets, or human hair) in suet feeders may entice titmice to nest nearby.

FEEDING: The Tufted Titmouse hunts for insects by hanging from twigs and branch tips. Sometimes it clings to trunks and peers into bark crevices. Hanging feeders, suet feeders mounted on tree trunks, and suet or peanut butter mix smeared onto trunks and branches are excellent methods of feeding. At the winter feeder, peanut kernels are its favorite food, with black-striped and gray-striped sunflower seed in second and third place. It will also eat oil-type sunflower seed, suet, nutmeats, and peanut butter mix.

PSALTRIPARUS MINIMUS

Bushtit

One of the smallest North American birds, the Bushtit travels in noisy, cheerful flocks most of the year.

Abundant water is the best way to attract this small bird. The Bushtit is a permanent resident throughout its range.

HABITAT: The Bushtit inhabits dense, deciduous streamside vegetation; woodland edges of maples and dogwoods; and chaparral, pinyon, juniper, and scrub oak woodlands. It often resides in western gardens with groves of deciduous trees and beds of shrubs, and a reliable source of water on the ground next to shrubs.

NESTING: The nest resembles a sack with an entrance hole near the top. It is often hung in plain sight in small trees or shrubs. Normally traveling in flocks, the Bushtit is paired and shy during breeding season.

FEEDING: Although it is mostly insectivorous, the Bushtit does occasionally eat berries and fruits, mostly of poison oak. There is some evidence that the insects inside leaf galls may be its chief food. Hopping and flitting about on leaves and twigs of shrubs and low trees, often in flocks of up to 50 individuals, it gleans enormous numbers of aphids, beetles, scale nits, leafhoppers, and many other small insects. It rarely takes food from feeding stations but may sample suet, suet mixes, and peanut butter.

SITTA CANADENSIS

Red-breasted Nuthatch

This active bird can often be seen moving head down on tree trunks, clinging with its stiff tail and sharp claws.

HABITAT: Prefers forests that have plenty of conifers, including mixed coniferous-deciduous forests. Mature stands of conifers attract this bird to the garden year-round.

NESTING: Generally digs its own nesting hole out of the soft, decaying wood of a dead tree, especially pine, aspen, birch, or fir. It often smears the entrance hole with sap, which may give its feathers a messy look. The Red-breasted Nuthatch also nests in woodpecker holes and in nest boxes hung on a tree trunk (preferably a dead tree) about 15 feet above the ground. Nests are loosely constructed; never open the nest box while it is occupied or everything may fall out.

FEEDING: Feeds mostly on seeds of conifers and on insects gleaned from the bark of tree trunks. It also sometimes feeds on the ground or while clinging to the seed heads of herbaceous plants such as ragweed or sunflowers. Nuthatches often store food for hard times. Attract them in winter with suet, peanut butter mix, peanut kernels, nutmeats, and sunflower seed.

The Red-breasted Nuthatch clings to pine cones and deftly extracts seeds. This one is eating peanut butter mix.

SITTA CAROLINENSIS

White-breasted Nuthatch

More common at feeders and more widespread than its red-breasted relative, this nuthatch is quite tame around feeders and can even be taught to accept food from human hands.

HABITAT: Found almost anywhere there are forests, in the West it inhabits pine forests as well as oak or juniper woodlands; in the East it prefers deciduous woods, especially those with beeches or oaks.

NESTING: Nests in the natural cavities and knotholes of dead trees or in abandoned woodpecker holes. Occasionally it excavates its own hole in the soft wood of dead or decaying trees. Oaks, elms, maples, apple, and other deciduous trees are prime candidates; pine trees are also used. The White-breasted Nuthatch often uses nest boxes mounted at least 12 feet up in a tree in a woodland setting.

FEEDING: Insects gleaned from the bark of tree trunks, and the nuts of deciduous trees (especially acorns and beechnuts) are principal natural foods. Often it stores food in fall under the loose bark of trees. It is a frequent visitor to winter feeders for suet and sunflower seed and also for peanut butter mix, nutmeats, and finely cracked corn.

The White-breasted Nuthatch creeps head down on trunks and holds its head at a 90-degree angle.

CERTHIA AMERICANA

Brown Creeper

The feeding behavior of this active, amusing bird is its hallmark; clinging to the trunks of trees and large limbs with its long, sharp claws, it spirals upward (never facing downward or sideways), probing the bark for insects until it nears the top of the tree. Then it flies down to the base of another tree to repeat the performance.

HABITAT: Found in nearly all types of forest, it is attracted to densely wooded gardens with large, mature trees. The shagbark hickory is an excellent tree to attract it.

NESTING: Sometimes the Brown Creeper nests in a natural cavity or an abandoned woodpecker hole in a dead tree. More often it builds its nest under loose, shaggy bark such as that found on dead trees and the live shagbark hickory. It is a difficult bird to entice into a nest box.

FEEDING: Most of the Brown Creeper's diet consists of insects gleaned from the bark of trees, although it does consume some nuts and seeds. In winter it enjoys peanut butter mix and suet mixes spread on the bark of trees, as well as chopped peanut kernels. It is often too timid to come to feeders when other birds are present.

Most populous in the northern parts of its range, the Brown Creeper is the only creeper in North America.

CAMPYLORHYNCHUS BRUNNEICAPILLUS

Cactus Wren

The Cactus Wren is the largest of all wrens, as big as a starling. Its home territory can include dozens of nests.

The Cactus Wren often takes up residence in gardens and around human habitations in the arid Southwest, where it is a permanent resident. **HABITAT:** Dense scrub along watercourses is a favorite home, along with sunny hillsides adjoining mesas and foothills. A chief requirement is plenty of prickly, thorny shrubs and cacti in which to nest. Cholla cactus, prickly pear, and cat's claw vine are favorites, but many other thorny plants are used. **NESTING:** The nest is shaped like a bottle with a crooked neck, with the narrow entrance hole and tunnel off to one side. It is often so deeply embedded in and surrounded with prickles and thorns that one wonders how the bird gets to it without injury. Occasionally this wren nests in woodpecker holes in trees or in cavities in old buildings. Each spring and summer new nests are built for each of two or three broods, but old ones are kept in repair for roosting. Cactus Wrens seldom use nest boxes. **FEEDING:** Most of this wren's food consists of insects it forages on the ground. Fruits of prickly pear and elderberry are important. Cactus Wrens visit feeders for suet, bread crumbs, and nutmeats. Watermelon is an especially prized offering.

THRYOTHORUS LUDOVICIANUS

Carolina Wren

Energetic song and perky habit make the Carolina Wren a much-loved bird of southeastern gardens.

This is the largest wren in its eastern range. It will nest in nearly any cavity available, from the pocket of a discarded coat to a lidless metal can. **HABITAT:** Brushy undergrowth is the favorite habitat of the Carolina Wren. It also inhabits rocky slopes with dense brush and thickets, shrubby forest edges and deeper undergrowth, and isolated groups of shrubs and trees in midwestern plains and moist lowlands. Woodland gardens with a dense understory of shrubs are most attractive. This bird is a permanent resident throughout its range; it is sometimes killed by cold weather at the northernmost fringes. **NESTING:** The Carolina Wren prefers cavities for nesting, although it sometimes nests in the crotches of trees. It is quite inventive about finding suitable cavities but will often use boxes built to the correct dimensions. It breeds from April to July and often raises two broods. **FEEDING:** Insects are the chief fare of the Carolina Wren. Only about 10 percent of its diet is plant food, and that is mostly in winter. Suet, peanut butter mix, sunflower seed, nutmeats, and corn bread will attract it to winter feeders. Offer food near shrubbery or brush piles.

TROGLODYTES AEDON

House Wren

The House Wren is distinguished by its small size and jaunty, wagging tail held at a 90-degree angle.

Common around human dwellings, this migratory bird is especially loved for its vivacious personality during breeding season. **HABITAT:** A resident of lowland deciduous woods and shrubby woodland edges and openings, the House Wren often takes up residence in gardens, particularly those with a backdrop of trees and shrubs surrounding a lawn or patio. **NESTING:** The early-arriving male constructs many trial nests in anticipation of attracting a mate. After a female selects a nest, she usually tears it apart and rebuilds it, often with the same materials. House Wrens build nests in cavities of astonishing variety, from old shoes to natural tree cavities and woodpecker holes. They readily nest in boxes and are among the few birds that will nest in a birdhouse or gourd dangling from a tree limb or a wire. Due to the male's prolific nest-building, a number of wren boxes in the garden are appreciated, although only one is eventually used. House Wrens are known to raid nests of competing cavity-nesting birds and pierce the eggs. **FEEDING:** House Wrens feed almost entirely on insects. Suet, corn bread, and white-bread crumbs may attract them to the feeder in spring and summer, although rarely.

TROGLODYTES TROGLODYTES

Winter Wren

Although similar to the House Wren in appearance, the Winter Wren is smaller and darker and usually has a shorter tail. It is also more secretive and less likely to frequent gardens.

HABITAT: The Winter Wren's chief habitat is the dark, shady undergrowth of coniferous forests, especially along steep, lush stream banks. Gardens most likely to attract this shy bird are those near large, mature coniferous forests and are themselves dense woodlands.

NESTING: The Winter Wren's nest is cunningly concealed on or near the ground, usually among the roots of a fallen tree, or under the roots of stumps, on stream banks or road cuts, and occasionally in abandoned buildings. Although most individuals are migratory, some remain in their harsh northern breeding range all year, so roosting boxes in winter are especially attractive. Winter Wrens have been known to use nest boxes placed low against the side of a shed or stump, but this is not common. Males usually build one or more decoy nests in the open.

FEEDING: This bird feeds almost exclusively on insects but may come to winter feeders for bread crumbs.

The Winter Wren is a shy woodland bird sometimes mistaken for a House Wren.

REGULUS CALENDULA

Ruby-crowned Kinglet

Among the smallest birds in North America, the Ruby-crowned Kinglet is the more likely kinglet to visit feeders in its southern winter range.

HABITAT: This bird seldom visits gardens in spring and summer, choosing dense coniferous forests instead. In winter it migrates to coastal and southern states, where deciduous and coniferous thickets and forest edges are its domain.

NESTING: The Ruby-crowned Kinglet nests in northern and high-altitude coniferous forests. It builds a hanging, globular nest, suspended from the tip of a branch high up in a spruce, fir, or other conifer.

FEEDING: Flitting from spot to spot, this tiny bird is well adapted to foraging on the delicate tips of branches for aphids, scales, and other tiny insects and their eggs. It is almost entirely insectivorous, although it occasionally eats a few nuts, seeds, or small fruits. It may visit small hanging feeders stocked with suet, peanut butter mix, and finely chopped nutmeats. A related species, the Golden-crowned Kinglet, is less likely to visit winter feeders. When it does it frequently joins chickadees in mixed flocks. It seldom nests near human dwellings.

The Ruby-crowned Kinglet often hovers in front of twigs and leaves as it inspects them for food.

SIALIA SIALIS

Eastern Bluebird

Competition for nesting cavities with the European Starling and House Sparrow has greatly reduced the population of this popular harbinger of spring.

HABITAT: Old fields with scattered trees and open, second-growth woodlands. Favorite spots include orchards, open farmland with a few trees, and fencerows. Rural gardens and orchards and suburban gardens near open farmland are ideal places to attract bluebirds.

NESTING: Bluebirds nest in cavities in trees and in woodpecker holes in trees and fence posts. They readily use nest boxes mounted on a post 4 to 5 feet from the ground, in full sun and away from human activity. Roadsides, pastures, and woodland edges facing open land are the best locations.

FEEDING: Bluebirds eat mostly insects; they perch on fence posts or small trees and fly down to eat on the grassy ground. They also eat the berries and fruits of dogwood, red cedar, sumac, bayberry, Virginia creeper, holly, blueberry, hackberry, and elderberry. Peanut butter mix, chopped dried fruit, mealworms, and chopped peanut kernels attract them to feeders in winter. The Western Bluebird is the western counterpart of the Eastern Bluebird, with similar habitat preferences. Attraction strategies for both species are virtually identical.

Providing nest boxes is an important way to help halt the decline of the Eastern Bluebird.

CATHARUS GUTTATUS

Hermit Thrush

The liquid notes of the Hermit Thrush are an unforgettable delight in the springtime woodland garden.

This is the only spotted thrush that winters in the United States, so it is the only one likely to visit winter feeders. During spring and summer, it is a shy, secretive bird of deep forests.

HABITAT: Deciduous woodlands and thickets, especially with berry bushes, are the winter habitats of this bird, and a dense cover of shrubs and trees is necessary to make it comfortable in the garden. In spring and summer, it moves to the more remote habitats of mixed deciduous-coniferous woods and purely coniferous forests. Especially in the Northwest, it nests at higher altitudes, often near timberline.

NESTING: A cup nest is usually built directly on the ground, under a small conifer or shrub, at the edge of woods.

FEEDING: In spring and summer, the Hermit Thrush feeds mostly on insects foraged on the ground. In winter plant foods constitute an important part of its diet, especially the fleshy fruits of poison ivy, holly, juniper, dogwood, serviceberry, sumac, and grape, with the addition of toyon, madrone, pepper tree, and poison oak in the West. At ground feeders and low platform feeders, it enjoys suet, peanut butter mix, nutmeats, raisins, sliced apple, and bakery crumbs.

Entice the American Robin to nest by making mud available and providing a nesting shelf.

TURDUS MIGRATORIUS

American Robin

Scarcely a garden in North America has not been visited at least a few times by this successful thrush.

HABITAT: A bird of woodland edges and openings, the American Robin needs open ground on which it can forage for food, and some woods or at least a few scattered trees and shrubs for nesting and roosting. Gardens with open lawns adjacent to woodlands, groves, and small trees and shrubs are ideal. Berry bushes are an attraction.

NESTING: Robins construct a cup nest that the female lines with mud by smearing it on the inner bowl with her breast. The nest is usually built in the crotch of a tree or shrub, anywhere from near the ground to as high as 50 feet. Windowsills and other ledges on human structures are also used, as well as special nesting shelves, as long as the site has a firm support and overhead protection from rain.

FEEDING: Robins forage in lawns for earthworms and eat many insects, caterpillars, and grubs. Fleshy fruits and berries are also important. Robins sometimes come to feeding stations for bread crumbs.

IXOREUS NAEVIUS

Varied Thrush

The rich, melancholy song of the Varied Thrush makes it especially treasured in the woodland garden.

The Varied Thrush of the Pacific Northwest is a shy woodland bird resembling a robin in size and form.

HABITAT: Inhabits the shady floor of deep, moist, coniferous forests, from the high slopes of the Cascades to the rain forests of the Pacific coast. Forested gardens with lots of mature conifers (especially firs), an understory of madrone and rhododendron, a forest floor carpeted with thick mosses, and numerous cranny-filled rocks and dripping waterfalls and streams are especially attractive. In winter this bird is often seen farther south in California, foraging on lawns with its relative the American Robin.

NESTING: The Varied Thrush constructs a cup nest of mosses, twigs, and mud on a horizontal branch of a small fir, spruce, hemlock, maple, or willow about 10 to 15 feet above the ground.

FEEDING: Primarily forages for insects and berries on the ground. Sometimes hunts earthworms in a manner similar to that of the American Robin. During winter it eats fruits of madrone, snowberry, juniper, brambles, buckthorn, poison oak, and pepper tree. In yards of the Northwest that are near coniferous woods, it comes to trays or ground feeders for millet and seed mix.

CHAMAEA FASCIATA

Wrentit

Seldom venturing more than a few feet out of brushy hiding spots, this shy western bird is more often heard than seen.

HABITAT: The Wrentit lives in dense, brushy, and preferably uninterrupted chaparral. Early in life it typically chooses a territory of about 2½ acres quite near that of its parents and seldom departs from it. The Wrentit hops about from bush to bush and almost never flies across open spaces larger than 30 feet.

Gardens with extensive areas of dense shrubs such as manzanita, coyote bush, and ceanothus are favored. Nearby hillsides of natural brush are a plus, as is a source of water located next to shrubby cover.

NESTING: The Wrentit nests in dense, twiggy shrubs and small trees, in thickets or solid brush.

FEEDING: Gleans many insects from the bark of shrubs and small trees, but fleshy fruits and berries constitute more than half its diet. Poison oak berries are a favorite food; the fruits of brambles, toyon, elderberry, sumac, and wax myrtle are also important. The Wrentit almost never feeds on the ground. It enjoys bread crumbs and may sample suet and peanut butter, but it will visit only those feeders that are located close to shrubby cover. It may feed from hummingbird or oriole nectar feeders.

The Wrentit builds small cup nests of plant fibers bound with spiderwebs.

DUMETELLA CAROLINENSIS

Gray Catbird

The Gray Catbird mimics the calls of other birds, but it is not nearly as accomplished as the Northern Mockingbird.

HABITAT: This bird resides in brushy thickets of shrubs and vines, preferably at streamsides and marshy forest edges but also at roadsides. It frequently resides close to houses in gardens and sometimes emerges from shrubbery to forage for insects in lawns. Human settlements have greatly expanded its range by increasing the areas of forest edges. It frequently visits birdbaths.

NESTING: The Gray Catbird's cup nest is generally placed low in a dense shrub, vine, or thicket at the margin of a stream or marsh or at a forest edge. Sometimes it is found in a low tree, especially a conifer. Garden shrubs such as deutzia, lilac, mock orange, and brambles are frequent nesting sites.

FEEDING: About half of the Gray Catbird's diet is insects. Fruits and berries that have fallen to the ground and been softened by moisture are its favorite plant foods, including fruits of brambles, cherries, holly, bayberry, and greenbrier. It frequents the feeding station in spring and summer for soft foods such as cooked breakfast cereal and steamed raisins, but it will also eat dried berries, chopped fresh fruit, cheese, peanut kernels, and bread and cracker crumbs.

The Gray Catbird is fearless around humans; it often comes close to someone imitating its catlike mew.

MIMUS POLYGLOTTOS

Northern Mockingbird

The Northern Mockingbird is famous for its expert mimicry of the calls of many other birds and mechanical noises.

HABITAT: Edges of woods next to open country, and fields and meadows with isolated shrubby thickets and groves of trees. Its three main habitat requirements are open, grassy ground for insect foraging, dense shrubs for nesting, and a high perch for singing and proclaiming its territory. Gardens are among its favorite dwelling places, especially if there are fruiting plants such as holly, Virginia creeper, hackberry, brambles, grape, pyracantha, cotoneaster, and fig.

NESTING: This bird builds cup nests in crotches or among the dense twigs of shrubs, low trees, or vines, usually about 5 to 10 feet above the ground. Low coniferous or broad-leaved evergreen trees are favorites, as are dense shrubs such as multiflora rose and bayberry.

FEEDING: While foraging in grassy areas for grasshoppers and beetles (its most important insect foods), the Northern Mockingbird often hitches its wings back and up. It visits feeders in summer and winter for suet, mealworms, bread crumbs, doughnuts, and both fresh and dried fruit, especially softened raisins, sliced apple, and oranges.

The Northern Mockingbird eats many insects; mealworms are a favorite treat at the feeder.

TOXOSTOMA RUFUM

Brown Thrasher

Although the shy Brown Thrasher eats many insects, berries are important food, especially in winter.

This shy, secretive bird sometimes nests in gardens. It occasionally mimics other birds and mechanical noises, whistling in short, staccato bursts.

HABITAT: The Brown Thrasher inhabits thickets and dry, brushy patches in old fields, woodland edges, and roadsides. It sometimes nests in gardens that have large, dense patches of shrubs and hedges.

NESTING: Low, thorny shrubs and low-branching prickly trees are favorite nesting spots. Greenbrier, gooseberry, hawthorn, honey locust, wild plum, and barberry are typical nesting plants. Resembling a basket, the large nest may even be placed directly on the ground.

FEEDING: The Brown Thrasher forages mostly on the ground under shrubs, picking up and tossing aside leaves and other debris to look for insects, grubs, fruits, and seeds. It eats many fruits and berries, especially in winter, including grapes, blackberries, wild cherries, dogwood berries, elderberries, blueberries, and bayberries. In many areas it will come readily to ground feeders and occasionally to low platform feeders, dashing out from shrubby cover for a quick bite. Scratch feed, cracked corn, and millet are favorite foods, along with bread crumbs, suet and suet mixtures, raisins, and oranges.

TOXOSTOMA REDIVIVUM

California Thrasher

The California Thrasher is a common resident of gardens, especially those with a reliable source of water.

The California Thrasher is an expert mimic known to imitate not only the sound of many other birds but also that of frogs, whistles, and the barks and howls of canines. Except when singing from the top of a shrub or low tree, it spends most of its time on the ground, generally preferring to run rather than fly from danger.

HABITAT: The California Thrasher inhabits dense scrub and chaparral on low mountain slopes and foothills and along streams. It lives only in California, where it is a permanent resident. Frequently it resides in gardens with plenty of shrub cover and low trees, especially when the soil under shrubs is well mulched with leaf litter and a reliable ground-level source of water is provided.

NESTING: Male and female together construct a loose cup nest of twigs and plant fibers close to the ground and deep within a dense, twiggy shrub or small tree.

FEEDING: Feeds on the ground under shrub cover, using its long, curved bill to rake leaf litter and probe and dig soil for insects, larvae, and spiders, as well as seeds, fruits, and berries that have fallen to the ground. It sometimes comes to the feeder for bread crumbs, mixed birdseed, raisins, and chopped fruit.

BOMBYCILLA CEDRORUM

Cedar Waxwing

About 90 percent of the Cedar Waxwing's diet consists of fleshy fruits, both wild and cultivated.

This beautiful crested bird often travels in flocks of 40 or more during the nonbreeding season. The Bohemian Waxwing is a larger Canadian relative.

HABITAT: Waxwings may appear anywhere there are abundant fleshy fruits on trees and shrubs. Their favorite habitats in the nonbreeding season include orchards, parks, forest edges, and second-growth woodlands along streams and rivers. In breeding season pairs seek out nesting territories near farm ponds and open woodlands. To attract them provide fruit-bearing plants and offer a reliable source of water.

NESTING: Gregarious by nature, these birds sometimes nest in loose colonies of a dozen or so pairs. They readily use wool, string, hair, and other materials set out by humans. They build cup nests in trees in a wide variety of situations.

FEEDING: Juniper berries are a favorite food, followed closely by the fruit of mountain ash, cherry, pyracantha, cotoneaster, dogwood, mistletoe, privet, apple, toyon, hawthorn, Russian olive, pepper tree, strawberry, and grape. Adults feed their young with insects. The birds are difficult to entice to the feeder, but once there, they eat large amounts of chopped or sliced apple, raisins, and currants.

VERMIVORA CELATA

Orange-crowned Warbler

This is one of the most common warblers in the West. It displays its orange crown when alarmed and during courtship. **HABITAT:** Prefers brushy thickets, especially along streams, near low marshes and swamps, and at forest edges and clearings. Gardens with dense shrubby areas and thick groves of aspen, poplar, and pine are most attractive, especially with a pool or stream nearby.

NESTING: The nest is large for a bird this size, a loose cup constructed of grasses and other plant fiber and lined with plant down and bits of fur and hair. A breeding pair usually builds it low in a shrub, 2 to 4 feet above the ground, often right next to a path, drive, or open, grassy area. Hedges and dense plantings of twiggy shrubs are prime garden locations.

FEEDING: Orange-crowned Warblers eat mostly insects they glean hanging from leaves at the ends of branches, although berries in winter are important fare. They occasionally come to feeders for peanut butter, suet, and doughnuts.

The Orange-crowned Warbler eats many scale insects, leafhoppers, leaf bugs, and aphids.

DENDROICA PETECHIA

Yellow Warbler

The cheery song and bright yellow coloration of the male Yellow Warbler make it a welcome visitor to many gardens. **HABITAT:** Preferred nesting habitats are thickets of alder, willow, elderberry, elm saplings, box elder, or dogwood next to streams and moist lowlands. Woodland edges, forest clearings of shrubby second growth, roadside hedges, fencerows, and patches of trees and shrubs in open country are also favored spots.

In the garden, hedges and shrub borders backed by trees on one side and open lawn and flowerbeds on the other are good nesting spots. Heavily planted yards with some parts left as tangled vegetation are best. Water, especially if in motion, is a definite plus.

NESTING: The Yellow Warbler often weaves its cup nest in the upright fork of a low shrub in a thicket, about 6 to 7 feet above the ground; but if tall streamside or floodplain trees are available, especially willows and cottonwoods, it may nest as high as 60 feet. Sunny woodland openings and edges are first choices for nesting.

FEEDING: Virtually the entire diet of Yellow Warblers consists of insects, especially caterpillars and other insect larvae. They rarely if ever visit feeding stations.

Often seen in breeding season and during migration, the Yellow Warbler winters from Mexico south to Brazil.

DENDROICA CORONATA

Yellow-rumped Warbler

This is the most common warbler to visit winter feeding stations, especially on the West Coast and in the Southeast. **HABITAT:** Yellow-rumped Warblers nest in the coniferous forests of mountains in the far north and seem to prefer the edges of mature forests where conifers mix with deciduous trees. In winter this bird may visit any kind of woodland, grove, open field, or shrubby hillside. In gardens, fruit-bearing plants are important, such as wax myrtle, bayberry, juniper, fig, dogwood, palmetto, laurel, Virginia creeper, elderberry, and grape.

NESTING: Often builds its nest on the horizontal limb of a tall conifer, especially pine, up to 50 feet above the ground. Sometimes nests in deciduous trees or thorny shrubs.

FEEDING: Feeds mainly on insects, but compared to other warblers, the Yellow-rumped Warbler eats quite a few berries in fall and winter, which explains its ability to survive farther north in winter. It may need a little coaxing to discover a feeder in winter; branches of its wild foods can alert it to your efforts. Once discovered, a feeder is likely to be visited regularly by more than one of these birds. Millet and other seeds, raisins, and grape jelly are favorite foods, as are suet, peanut butter mix, and bakery crumbs.

The Yellow-rumped Warbler is more likely to be seen in winter, when its habitat needs are less specific.

GEOTHLYPIS TRICHAS

Common Yellowthroat

The male Common Yellowthroat is protective of its low-lying nest.

Although this is one of the most common warblers in North America, it prefers wild places. A nesting pair in the garden is an unusual treasure.

HABITAT: Thorny thickets, tangled weeds, and thick grassy or reedy areas next to marshes, streamsides, and rural roads are preferred habitats of the Common Yellowthroat. It spends most of its time on or near the ground, except when the male perches on top of cattails or a shrub to sing. Appropriate habitat is the best way to attract this bird. Gardens with low-lying boggy areas or with marshes, swamps, or other wet ground nearby are most likely to attract it.

NESTING: Rather large nests are constructed of plant fibers, grass stalks, and bark on or close to the ground, up to as much as 3 feet high in dense weeds, grasses, cattails, or shrubs. Males can be quite aggressive when protecting their territory during breeding season.

FEEDING: The Common Yellowthroat is primarily an insect eater, foraging for ants, aphids, leafhoppers, and spiders from low-lying leaves and stems and sometimes snapping up grasshoppers and flying insects. They are not known to visit bird feeders.

PIRANGA OLIVACEA

Scarlet Tanager

Scarlet Tanagers spend most of their time high in treetops, but they also forage in shrubs and on the ground.

Shy and difficult to detect when it is lurking high in trees, this brightly colored bird may occasionally be enticed down to bird feeders and garden pools.

HABITAT: This is a bird of dense, mature forests. Tall oaks, tulip trees, hickories, ashes, hemlocks and pines are favorite trees. Occasionally it visits gardens; those with a dense woodland habitat or mature forests close by are best. It migrates to South America for the winter.

NESTING: The Scarlet Tanager's nest is a shallow cup of twigs, pine needles, and fibrous plant material built on a horizontal branch of a deciduous tree up to 75 feet above the ground. Oaks are among its favored nesting trees.

FEEDING: Tanagers are mostly insect eaters but do eat fleshy fruits. Serviceberries, mulberries, grapes, blueberries, and brambles are among their favorite garden plants. They occasionally visit summer feeders for sliced apple, orange, and banana; raisins; bakery crumbs; nutmeats; and peanut butter mix. They are also known to take sugar water from nectar feeders. They prefer second-story window feeders and platform feeders raised high off the ground, but they can be persuaded to use lower feeding stations, even those on the ground.

PIPILO ERYTHROPHTHALMUS

Eastern Towhee

Plant understory shrubs and mulch them with a carpet of fallen leaves to attract the Eastern Towhee.

The Eastern Towhee is an asset in the garden for its cheerful music and color. The Spotted Towhee is its western equivalent. Both were formerly known as the Rufous-sided Towhee.

HABITAT: In the wild the Eastern Towhee prefers shrubby forest edges, thickets, and old fields. The Spotted Towhee is found in chaparral and juniper-pinyon woodlands and along streams. In gardens both species prefer dense, evergreen thickets and hedges, and brush piles. Plenty of leaf litter under shrubs is important. Towhees often reside in suitable gardens year-round.

NESTING: Towhees prefer to nest on the ground or close to it, under a shrub or brush pile. They sometimes nest higher up in a shrub, vine, or tree. Serviceberry, elderberry, and blueberry are favorite garden plants.

FEEDING: Towhees scratch vigorously with both feet at once as they forage on the ground, usually under the cover of a shrub. Seeds and insects are primary foods. They visit summer and winter feeders for sunflower seed, mixed birdseed, nutmeats, niger, millet, finely cracked corn, and suet. They prefer feeding on the ground under a feeder, close to cover. On elevated feeders their furious scratching sends seeds flying in all directions.

PIPILO FUSCUS

Canyon Towhee

This desert resident and the California Towhee were once thought to be the same species, the Brown Towhee. They are similar birds.

HABITAT: The Canyon Towhee resides in washes, lowlands, canyons, and hills of the desert Southwest dominated by cactus and mesquite; juniper-pinyon woodlands; and some higher plateaus with scrub oaks and juniper. Where the ranges of the Canyon Towhee and the Spotted Towhee overlap, the Canyon Towhee feeds lower in shrubs and trees, the Spotted Towhee higher. Desert gardens with open shrubs and cactus and a dependable source of water on the ground are most attractive.

NESTING: The Canyon Towhee builds large nests of twigs, grasses, and animal hair in a twiggy crotch from 3 to 12 feet off the ground in a dense shrub or low tree.

FEEDING: Like the Eastern Towhee, this bird feeds mostly on the ground, although it doesn't scratch as vigorously. Sometimes it forages for fruits in the low branches of a shrub or cactus. It will visit the bird feeder on the ground or a low platform for fresh fruit, mixed birdseed, finely cracked corn, millet, niger, and sunflower seed.

Half an orange offered low in a shrub is a good way to attract the Canyon Towhee.

PIPILO CRISSALIS

California Towhee

This rather plain-looking bird is a common resident of gardens of the West Coast. It lurks under shrubs, parked cars, and other cover, emerging to feed on lawns or pavement or under feeders. It often shows little fear of humans. This is surprising, because in the wild this bird is timid. Even when it is not in sight, however, its territorial call, a sharp, metallic "chink," alerts us to its presence.

HABITAT: Preferred habitats of the California Towhee include low shrub in chaparral. Gardens with plenty of dense, low shrubs, a pool or ground-level birdbath, and a ground-level feeding station are attractive to this bird.

NESTING: The California Towhee usually builds its cup nest in the densest part of a twiggy shrub or low tree, from 3 to 12 feet above the ground. Animal hair is a suitable nesting material to offer.

FEEDING: This bird is a ground-feeder, scratching for the seeds of weeds and grasses under shrubs and in dense, grassy patches. It often comes to bird feeders for fruit and seeds, especially hulled oats, millet, finely cracked corn, niger, and sunflower seed.

The California Towhee feeds mostly on the ground, so offer food on the ground or on low platforms.

SPIZELLA ARBOREA

American Tree Sparrow

Along with the White-throated Sparrow, this is one of the most common true sparrows to visit winter feeding stations in the Northeast. In spring and summer, it retires to the tundra to breed. The name is misleading, as it spends little time in trees.

HABITAT: In winter small flocks roam about weedy fields, marshes, roadsides, and forest edges. Open lawn and large flowerbeds gone to seed are the best places to feed this bird in winter.

NESTING: The American Tree Sparrow leaves the northern states for its Arctic breeding grounds in late March and April. It nests in brushy thickets of willow and other shrubs at the tree line in Alaska and northern Canada.

FEEDING: This bird generally eats on the ground in the wild, vigorously scratching for the weed seeds that make up most of its diet. It may also cling to weed tops, pecking for seeds. At feeding stations it can be fed either on the ground or on low platforms, as well as hanging feeders. White and red proso millet and finely cracked corn are its preferred foods, along with suet. It will sometimes eat canary seed and, to a lesser extent, black-striped sunflower seed.

The American Tree Sparrow is most apt to visit the garden during the harshest, snowiest weather.

SPIZELLA PASSERINA

Chipping Sparrow

The Chipping Sparrow is fearful of other birds, which often drive it away from feeders.

This small bird is most frequently seen in most of North America in spring and summer, and in the southeastern states at winter feeders. It is often surprisingly tame around humans.
HABITAT: Lives in grassy woodland clearings and edges and borders of meadows, streams, lakes, and ponds. Open lawn with scattered trees and shrubs bordered by flowerbeds and with a perimeter of trees farther off makes a fine garden habitat.
NESTING: The Chipping Sparrow generally builds its cup nest on the limb of a conifer, sometimes as low as a foot off the ground, but more often higher up, to 50 feet. Deciduous trees, shrubs, and vines may also be used, and bayberry shrubs are preferred nesting site.
FEEDING: In spring and summer, insects make up most of this sparrow's diet. But especially in fall and winter, it eats grass seeds and small weed seeds in great quantities. Millet and canary seed are popular at winter feeders, along with bakery crumbs. Sunflower seed may occasionally be eaten. Ground-feeding is best, although when no other birds are around, it may hop onto low platform feeders. To decrease the effects of competition on this nonaggressive bird, broadcast food over a wide area.

PASSERELLA ILIACA

Fox Sparrow

The Fox Sparrow is seldom found far from dense, brushy cover. It often nests at moist, boggy streamsides.

Many consider the haunting melody of this bird the most elegant song of all sparrows.
HABITAT: Prefers dense thickets and brushy woodlands, often near moist, boggy areas and streamsides but also on drier slopes. Woodland gardens with thick, tangled shrubs and vines near low, moist soil and seeps are attractive. Knotweed, grape, elderberry, and blueberry are favorite garden plants for food; shrub willows, spruce, ceanothus, alder, and spruce are preferred cover plants, especially for nesting.
NESTING: Builds a cup of twigs, moss, and other plant fibers lined with grass, feathers, and animal hair. The nest is constructed on or near the ground, in the low branches of a spruce, or in a willow thicket. It is often at the edge of a bog or stream but sometimes on a dry slope.
FEEDING: The Fox Sparrow feeds mostly on seeds and fruits it finds by vigorously scratching, both feet at once, on the ground close to or under shrubs. Sometimes it eats insects it turns up in the process. In winter it forages on the ground beneath feeders over and over again for millet and mixed birdseed, bits of suet, nutmeats, and bakery crumbs. Sometimes it scratches on snow energetically enough to dig through to the soil below.

MELOSPIZA MELODIA

Song Sparrow

The bright, cheerful music of the Song Sparrow makes it a much sought-after resident of gardens.

In many parts of its range, the Song Sparrow may be a permanent resident. In the Deep South, it is a winter visitor.
HABITAT: Inhabits thickets near water in both summer and winter, as well as drier areas along fencerows, old fields, roadsides, and, in the plains states, open groves with dense undergrowth. Best gardens are not overly neat and tidy. Brush piles and dense patches of shrubs next to flowerbeds are appropriate habitats. Provide water nearby, as this bird loves to bathe and drink often. High singing perches are essential to the male during breeding season.
NESTING: First brood is raised in neat cups woven of grass and hidden in a weedy patch on or close to the ground. For the next one or two broods, the nest is often built about 4 feet high in a brush pile or low shrub or tree such as barberry but also red cedar, alder, or yew. It occasionally uses nesting shelves of correct size, mounted on the wall of a shed or house 2 to 4 feet above the ground, behind dense shrubs.
FEEDING: Frequently visits feeders in all seasons, but especially in winter, for millet, mixed birdseed, sunflower seed, niger, bread crumbs, and finely cracked corn. It prefers eating on the ground, although it will often visit elevated feeders.

ZONOTRICHIA ALBICOLLIS

White-throated Sparrow

This familiar winter visitor to feeders in the East is treasured for its beautiful song, which it often performs in winter.

HABITAT: In winter this sparrow prefers brushy streamsides, where it scratches for the seeds of weeds and grasses. It summers in the openings and edges of coniferous and mixed woodlands of the far northeastern United States and in Canada. In the garden ideal spots include dense patches of shrubbery and hedges next to open, grassy areas.

NESTING: In dense thickets and woodland margins of its northern breeding grounds, the White-throated Sparrow builds a grassy cup nest on or near the ground.

FEEDING: This sparrow comes only rarely to elevated feeders, preferring to feed on the ground near the close cover of shrubs. In the wild it feeds primarily on small seeds. At feeders its tastes are similar to those of the White-crowned Sparrow, although it takes more readily to finely cracked corn, enjoying it almost as much as red proso millet. Its favorite foods are hulled sunflower seed (often gleaned from the shells left by other birds) and white proso millet. Niger seed is readily taken.

The White-throated Sparrow often performs its beautiful song in winter. It spends summers in the far north.

ZONOTRICHIA LEUCOPHRYS

White-crowned Sparrow

Sometimes thought of as a western bird, this handsome sparrow also inhabits the eastern United States in winter, where it frequently visits feeders.

HABITAT: Far-ranging in winter, for nesting this bird prefers brushy thickets at the edges of forests bordering streams, ponds, marshes, and other watery places. Gardens with good shrub cover and ample water are especially appropriate, both summer and winter.

NESTING: Usually builds its grassy cup nest on or near the ground in a patch of grasses and weeds under a shrub. Sometimes it nests in small conifers or twiggy deciduous trees up to 25 feet above the ground. Grassy, open places and shrubby cover are the two nesting essentials.

FEEDING: Eats mostly small seeds, but in late spring and summer also eats a wide variety of insects. It prefers ground-feeding at the winter feeder and is easily driven off by more aggressive birds. Peanut kernels and hulled sunflower seed are its favorite foods, but white proso millet is almost as popular, followed by oil-type and black-striped sunflower seed, peanut hearts, red proso millet, flax, milo, and finely cracked corn. It will also eat sliced apple.

Many consider the White-crowned Sparrow to be the handsomest sparrow to visit the garden.

JUNCO HYEMALIS

Dark-eyed Junco

Aptly nicknamed "snowbirds," these birds visit most of the United States in winter, when flocks of them are common on the ground under feeders.

HABITAT: Juncos nest in the coniferous or mixed forests of the mountainous United States and Canada. They prefer the edges of woods bordering a stream, pond, lake, trail, or mountain meadow. Woodland roadsides and the edges of cut-over clearings are also attractive. In winter they migrate south or to lower elevations and roam about in flocks. Forest edges and brushy fields are their favorite winter haunts, along with roadsides, hedges, parks, and gardens. Open ground and flowerbeds gone to seed are favorite garden attractions, especially if backed by a woodland.

NESTING: Builds a grassy nest on or near the ground at a forest edge, preferably close to water, or in a forest with dense groundcover.

FEEDING: Eats mostly seeds, but in spring and summer it also eats many insects or feeds them to its young. Strongly prefers ground-feeding but may occasionally alight on low platform feeders. Red proso millet is its favorite food at winter feeders, followed by white proso millet, canary seed, finely cracked corn, and oil-type sunflower seed. Suet, peanut butter mix, peanut hearts, and bakery products are also eaten.

The Dark-eyed Junco is sometimes called "snowbird" because it is most seen at feeders during bad weather.

CARDINALIS CARDINALIS

Northern Cardinal

The Northern Cardinal commonly nests in gardens that offer plenty of fruit-bearing shrubs.

The Northern Cardinal is possibly the most popular and well-known bird in the eastern United States.

HABITAT: In the East this bird is found in thickets and brambles along streams, in open woods, and at the edges of forests and fields. In the Southwest it inhabits mesquite thickets and mixed woodland edges along washes and streams. Hedges and shrubs adjacent to lawn or drive backed by a mix of coniferous and deciduous trees are frequent nest sites. Preferred plants include sumac, brambles, cherry, dogwood, grape, mulberry, blueberry, Russian olive, tulip tree, elderberry, and hackberry.

NESTING: Cup nests are firmly attached to the forks of small branches in thickets or vines 2 to 12 feet off the ground, or in dense thickets of young saplings. Young evergreens, brambles, honeysuckle thickets, and dense tangles of thorny shrubs such as roses, hollies, and barberries are ideal sites.

FEEDING: The Northern Cardinal eats primarily seeds and berries, although it consumes many insects during breeding season. At feeders it prefers unhulled sunflower seed over all other foods, offered on or near the ground. It also eats safflower seed, white proso millet, bread, nutmeats, and peanut butter mix.

PHEUCTICUS LUDOVICIANUS

Rose-breasted Grosbeak

Most Rose-breasted Grosbeaks spend the winter in Mexico and South America.

Striking colors and fondness for nesting in gardens make this species popular in the Midwest and Northeast.

HABITAT: Thickets of saplings and shrubs where deciduous forests open onto rivers, streams, swamps, old fields, pastures, and clearings are preferred habitats. It often takes to overgrown orchards and frequently nests in gardens with abundant water, dense plantings of small trees, shrubs, and hedges, and a perimeter of mature woodland.

NESTING: The loosely woven nest is usually located close to water in a thicket of shrubs or saplings, such as alders or young oaks, in a branch crotch 8 to 20 feet above the ground. Horsehair is an acceptable nesting material to offer.

FEEDING: Eats large numbers of harmful insects and is a boon around the garden or orchard. Also eats seeds and flower buds foraged in the tops of trees, especially elms, hickories, and beeches, and the seeds and pits of fruits, especially elderberry and wild cherry. Unfortunately, this bird is especially fond of garden peas. At the summer feeder and especially before migration in fall, it readily accepts sunflower seed. Mixed birdseed and suet may also be eaten. Water for drinking is a strong attraction.

PASSERINA AMOENA

Lazuli Bunting

The Lazuli Bunting occasionally visits ground feeders or low platform feeders during its migrations.

A western bird of plains and mountains, the Lazuli Bunting is most likely to visit feeders when migrating to and from its winter range in Mexico.

HABITAT: This bird is found in moist, low-lying thickets of the prairies and western plains, and woodland streamside thickets of aspen, alder, cottonwood and willow in mountain valleys and canyons. It also inhabits drier hillsides and even sage and open scrub. To be most attractive, a garden should have thick plantings of shrubs (especially roses and brambles), a meadow or flowerbed with tall grasses and flowers, and running water nearby. Utility wires, medium-size trees, or other high perches are necessary for it to stake out territory with its beautiful song.

NESTING: The Lazuli Bunting builds a coarse cup of grass low in a twiggy shrub, small tree, or vine. Offering animal hair can sometimes be an inducement to nesting.

FEEDING: The Lazuli Bunting feeds on insects and seeds that it forages on or close to the ground around shrubs or in grassy areas. At the bird feeder in fall and spring, it favors mixed birdseed containing millet. Ground feeders are preferred, although the Lazuli Bunting can be enticed onto a low platform.

PASSERINA CYANEA

Indigo Bunting

In the sunlight the plumage of this bird is a deep, brilliant blue, but in shade it may appear black. It is most frequently seen at feeding stations in spring, summer, and fall; most Indigo Buntings migrate to Central and South America for the winter.

HABITAT: The Indigo Bunting is found in open, brushy fields and pastures, forest edges, and brushy clearings. It also favors thickets along the margins of rivers and streams. It occasionally nests in gardens that have dense stands of shrubs and hedges. It tends to live in more outlying suburban and rural areas but is becoming increasingly common in suburban gardens.

NESTING: Dense stands of young saplings and thickets of shrubs, especially thorny canebrakes of raspberries and blackberries, are prime spots for this bird's nest, a cup tightly woven of plant fibers, hair, bits of paper, and even snakeskin.

FEEDING: This seedeater is especially fond of the seeds of thistle, goldenrod, aster, grasses, and grains. It also eats insects captured in trees and shrubs or on the ground. Unhulled sunflower seed is a favorite food at feeding stations, but it also eats millet, canary seed, nutmeats, and occasionally fruits.

The Indigo Bunting prefers ground-feeding but can be enticed onto low platforms and even hanging feeders.

ICTERUS SPURIUS

Orchard Oriole

Similar to a small (bluebird-size) robin, this oriole has a reddish-brown breast and body with a black head, back, wings, and tail. It frequently nests in loose colonies in fruit trees, where it destroys many harmful pests.

HABITAT: Like the Baltimore Oriole, the Orchard Oriole frequently nests in trees overhanging rivers and streams. It often lives in orchards, where it finds plentiful insects and the few fruits that it eats, and in shade and street trees in suburban areas.

NESTING: The Orchard Oriole hangs its tightly woven, pendulous nest from the tip of a tree branch, sometimes in scattered colonies. It breeds from April to July.

FEEDING: More than 90 percent of the Orchard Oriole's diet is insects, although it occasionally eats a few fruits. Mulberries are a favorite, as are brambles, blueberries, and cherries. The best way to attract this shy bird down from the trees for regular visits through the summer is to offer sugar water in a nectar feeder specially designed for orioles. Lure it to the nectar feeder by offering a highly visible display of halved orange and apple nearby.

The Orchard Oriole is worth the few fruits it might eat for the many pest insects it consumes in fruit trees.

ICTERUS GALBULA

Baltimore Oriole

Mostly migratory and known as a summer visitor, the Baltimore Oriole has been staying north in increasing numbers.

HABITAT: Prefers tall shade trees with shrubby undergrowth, often in lowlands near streams and along country roads but also in open woods and orchards. Often nests in gardens and street trees in suburban areas, especially in ornamental trees such as the American elm that are native to floodplain habitats.

NESTING: Weaves a pendulous, sack-shaped nest suspended from the tip of branch in a tall tree, such as elm, cottonwood, or maple, often over a river, street, or drive. String, horsehair, and other nesting material offered in pieces no longer than 8 inches are major attractions.

FEEDING: Eats primarily insects (especially caterpillars) but also fleshy fruits and berries. Mulberries, serviceberries, brambles, cherries, mountain ash, nuts, and figs are among its favorite plant foods. It sometimes visits the summer feeder for chopped and halved fruit and grape and apple jelly, and will visit a hummingbird feeder if there is enough of a perch. It is quite fond of sugar water offered in specially designed oriole feeders. Occasional overwintering individuals accept millet and suet from winter feeders.

Oranges, apples, and pears halved and firmly attached are good for attracting the Baltimore Oriole.

CARPODACUS PURPUREUS
Purple Finch

The Purple Finch is almost entirely vegetarian, although it may feed a few caterpillars to its young.

The Purple Finch is a frequent visitor to feeding stations in winter and often breeds in summer gardens.

HABITAT: Breeds in northern coniferous or mixed coniferous-deciduous forests, especially around the openings of swamps, streams, and logged-over clearings. At breeding time it is likely to be attracted to a group of conifers, especially firs and spruces, at the edge of a garden woodland, particularly if water is available. In winter the Purple Finch usually travels in flocks throughout a wide range of habitats.

NESTING: The Purple Finch builds its shallow cup nest well out on the limb of a conifer, frequently as high as 60 feet above the ground. Firs, spruces, pines, and redwoods are popular residences; box elder, ash, and dogwood may also be used.

FEEDING: Eats mostly leaf and flower buds, soft fruits, and seeds. Favorite food plants include fir, maple, birch, ash, sweet gum, juniper, tupelo, mulberry, dogwood, and pyracantha. At feeders it takes sunflower seed, especially the oil type, and, to a lesser extent, mixed birdseed, niger, and nutmeats. It comes to all kinds of feeders but prefers them high off the ground; second-story window trays are ideal.

CARPODACUS MEXICANUS
House Finch

A source of water for bathing and drinking is important in habitats attractive to the House Finch.

Both in its native western range and in the East (where it was introduced in the 1940s by cage-bird dealers), the House Finch has adapted to human settlements in much the same way as the House Sparrow. It is less aggressive, however, and has a prettier song and brighter coloration.

HABITAT: A resident of chaparral, brushy deserts, and old fields, this bird is widely adapted to areas around buildings and is a frequent garden resident.

NESTING: Highly adaptable, it has been known to nest in cavities, but prefers to nest in a tree, shrub, cactus, or vine on a building. It will even nest in a hanging basket, or on the ground. Gregarious all year, it nests in colonies and travels in flocks in the nonbreeding season.

FEEDING: Eats mostly weed seeds but is fond of soft fruits, regularly extracting and eating seeds from winter berries. In the West just about any type of feeder and any type of food are attractive, including suet, all types of birdseed, most fruits, bakery crumbs, kitchen scraps, and even nectar at hummingbird feeders. At eastern feeders it eats mainly birdseed. Sunflower, niger, white proso millet, and canary seed are favorites, in that order.

CARDUELIS FLAMMEA
Common Redpoll

Hailing from northern Canada, the Common Redpoll sometimes visits winter feeders in the United States.

In "invasion" years huge flocks of these far northern finches descend into the United States. They are quite fearless of humans.

HABITAT: Most at home in the southern tundra and coniferous forests of the far north, this and the Hoary Redpoll are reported to survive lower temperatures than any other songbird. In winter large flocks range over a wide variety of habitats, from grasslands to shrubby open land to forest. Open woodland gardens with coniferous trees (especially pine and larch), deciduous trees such as birch, aspen, willow, and elm, and areas of tall grass and flowers that have been allowed to go to seed are most attractive. Lilac is an attractive shrub for food. Redpolls are known to bathe in snow and icy streams.

NESTING: Nests in forest openings and swamps in northern Canada, where it builds a loose cup on a platform of sticks and twigs 3 to 6 feet high in a tree or shrub.

FEEDING: In winter eats mostly seeds, feeding on the ground and by clinging to the tops of weeds and grasses projecting above the snow. At winter feeders offer nutmeats and suet, and sunflower, niger, and millet seed. Feed on the ground, on platforms, and in hanging feeders.

CARDUELIS PINUS

Pine Siskin

Pine Siskins apparently use House Sparrows to alert them to feeders, then drive the House Sparrows off for the winter. Pine Siskins are remarkably tame around humans.

HABITAT: Usually nests on the edges of coniferous forests and in logged-over, second-growth forest clearings in the mountains and the North. In winter it roams about in large flocks. Best garden habitats resemble woodland edges opening onto grassy areas, with flowerbeds allowed to go to seed. Alder, birch, spruce, pine, sweet gum, and maple are favorite food plants.

NESTING: Often nesting in loose colonies, the Pine Siskin builds its cup nest on the outer stretches of horizontal conifer limbs about 10 feet above the ground. Pines and hemlocks are frequent choices.

FEEDING: Typically feeds on tall weeds and tree branches, tearing the seed heads apart, then dropping to the ground to eat. Niger, hulled sunflower, and black-oil sunflower seed are favorites at hanging feeders or scattered on the ground. It may also sample canary seed, millet, finely cracked corn, and suet.

The Pine Siskin is uncommon at feeders, but when it appears it's often in flocks of up to 200 birds.

CARDUELIS TRISTIS

American Goldfinch

The American Goldfinch is quite sociable in winter, when it is apt to visit feeders in hungry flocks of 30 or more birds.

HABITAT: Especially when nesting, this bird is seldom found far from thistles. Weedy fields, orchards, meadows with a few scattered trees, openings in forests, and brushy old fields are preferred. In winter it roams in nearly all types of open terrain. Providing water is an excellent way to attract this bird, as it loves to bathe. Water in motion is especially attractive.

NESTING: Hedges and shrubs near grassy, weedy meadows are preferred nesting sites. The nest is a cup of plant fibers and thistledown woven so tightly that it will hold water. Sometimes it is built in a small tree or in a patch of thistles.

FEEDING: Especially in winter, diet consists mostly of weed seeds and the hard, dry seeds of trees. Food plants include serviceberry, birch, hornbeam, sweet gum, mulberry, hemlock, elm, and alder. At the feeder hulled sunflower seed and pieces are preferred, followed by niger seed, then unhulled sunflower seed, especially the oil type, and mixed birdseed. Hanging feeders are best, although it will visit all types of feeders, including ground feeders.

The American Goldfinch lends cheer to the garden as it flashes around seeking insects and seeds.

COCCOTHRAUSTES VESPERTINUS

Evening Grosbeak

During the nonbreeding season this highly social bird often wanders in sizable flocks throughout its range.

HABITAT: Dense coniferous and mixed deciduous-coniferous forests are preferred, although this bird is expanding into a variety of habitats, perhaps due to the increased landscape use of maples and the increased availability of sunflower seed at feeders. Mature spruces, firs, and maples, especially box elder, make a garden attractive. Water for drinking is appreciated.

NESTING: Builds a shallow cup of twigs usually at the twiggy end of a conifer branch as high as 70 feet off the ground, or sometimes in a deciduous tree such as willow, maple, ash, birch, or oak.

FEEDING: In summer this bird eats many insects, but in other seasons nearly all of its food is vegetable, especially maple seeds and dogwood berries, but also the seeds of pine, spruce, serviceberry, snowberry, cherry, mountain ash, hackberry, juniper, fir, manzanita, and Russian olive. At the feeder it loves sunflower seed, which a flock will consume in vast quantities on cold days, and will eat little else. It prefers high platform feeders but readily takes food offered from low platforms or even on the ground.

When flocks of Evening Grosbeaks arrive, offer them food in several feeders to avoid squabbling.

A pair of binoculars kept handy at your favorite viewing window will bring birds up close for better observation. A pair of 7×35 or 8×40 binoculars will give you a good view. Modestly priced brands are fine for beginners.

ADDITIONAL RESOURCES

AIDS TO IDENTIFICATION
A field guide is essential for bird identification. Look for a sturdily bound guide with full descriptions, color illustrations that point out distinguishing marks, and range maps. Good choices are:
- *National Geographic Field Guide to the Birds of North America,* by Jon L. Dunn (National Geographic Society, 1999)
- *A Field Guide to the Birds: A Completely New Guide to All the Birds of Eastern and Central North America,* by Roger Tory Peterson (Houghton Mifflin, 1998)
- *A Field Guide to Western Birds,* by Roger Tory Peterson (Houghton Mifflin, 1990)

JOINING WITH OTHERS
Share your interest in birds through local and national clubs, birding magazines, and online sites. Many local clubs sponsor field trips and programs. Check the phone book, or call a nearby nature center to find your local chapter of the National Audubon Society. Or contact the national headquarters:
- National Audubon Society, 700 Broadway, New York, NY 10003
  Online: www.audubon.org

To contribute to knowledge about feeder birds, join Project FeederWatch, a study of feeder-bird populations continent-wide and other feeder-related subjects. The annual Great Backyard Bird Count is another way for you to contribute to science. Contact:
- The Cornell Lab of Ornithology, 159 Sapsucker Woods Rd., Ithaca, NY 14850
  Online: www:birds.cornell.edu

To make your yard more inviting to birds, participate in the Backyard Wildlife Habitat Program of the National Wildlife Federation, designed for properties of all sizes. Your yard can be certified if it meets requirements for food, water, and shelter. Contact:
- The National Wildlife Federation, Backyard Wildlife Habitat Program, 8925 Leesburg Pike, Vienna, VA 22184-0001
  Online: www.nwf.org/habitats

Birding magazines will keep you informed on techniques of attracting birds and others' experiences. Choices include:
- *Bird Watcher's Digest,* P.O. Box 110, Marietta, OH 45750
  Online: www.birdwatchersdigest.com

- *Birder's World,* P.O. Box 1612, Waukesha, WI 53187-1612
  Online: www.birdersworld.com
- *Birding* and *North American Birds,* the American Birding Association, P.O. Box 6599, Colorado Springs, CO 80934
  Online: www.americanbirding.org
- *The Bird's-Eye reView,* National Bird-Feeding Society, P.O. Box 23L, Northbrook, IL 60065-0023
  Online: www.birdfeeding.org
- *WildBird,* Circulation, 3 Burroughs, Irvine, CA 92618
  Online: www.animalnetwork.com

EQUIPMENT AND SUPPLIES
Many companies, large and small, sell feeders, houses, and other supplies by mail. The feeders and birdbaths shown on pages 42, 44, 45, and 52 are available from:
- Duncraft, 102 Fisherville Rd., Concord, NH 03303-2086
  Online: www.duncraft.com

Other long-established sources of high-quality products include:
- Droll Yankees, 27 Mill Rd., Foster, RI 02825
  Online: www.drollyankees.com
- Wild Birds Unlimited, 270 stores nationwide.
  Online: www.wbu.com

INDEX

A number in boldface indicates
a photograph or illustration.
An asterisk following a number (*)
indicates a descriptive entry in the
"Gallery of Birds."

METRIC CONVERSIONS

U.S. Units to Metric Equivalents			Metric Units to U.S. Equivalents		
To Convert From	Multiply By	To Get	To Convert From	Multiply By	To Get
Inches	25.4	Millimeters	Millimeters	0.0394	Inches
Inches	2.54	Centimeters	Centimeters	0.3937	Inches
Feet	30.48	Centimeters	Centimeters	0.0328	Feet
Feet	0.3048	Meters	Meters	3.2808	Feet
Yards	0.9144	Meters	Meters	1.0936	Yards
Square inches	6.4516	Square centimeters	Square centimeters	0.1550	Square inches
Square feet	0.0929	Square meters	Square meters	10.764	Square feet
Square yards	0.8361	Square meters	Square meters	1.1960	Square yards
Acres	0.4047	Hectares	Hectares	2.4711	Acres
Cubic inches	16.387	Cubic centimeters	Cubic centimeters	0.0610	Cubic inches
Cubic feet	0.0283	Cubic meters	Cubic meters	35.315	Cubic feet
Cubic feet	28.316	Liters	Liters	0.0353	Cubic feet
Cubic yards	0.7646	Cubic meters	Cubic meters	1.308	Cubic yards
Cubic yards	764.55	Liters	Liters	0.0013	Cubic yards

To convert from degrees Fahrenheit (F) to degrees Celsius (C), first subtract 32, then multiply by ⁵⁄₉.

To convert from degrees Celsius to degrees Fahrenheit, multiply by ⁹⁄₅, then add 32.